Our feast is, literally, a feast of bold colours and generous gestures. It is driven by an unapologetic desire to celebrate food and its virtues, to display abundance in the same way that a market stallholder does: show everything you've got and shout its praise whole heartedly.

We got started in July 2002, not really sure what was ahead of us, when we opened Ottolenghi – food shop, patisserie, deli, restaurant, bakery. A place with no single description but at the same time a crystal-clear reflection of our obsessive relationship with food. In a small shop in Notting Hill we began to cook and bake.

We did it while the white paint on the walls was still drying. Together with a small group of friends, and alongside some newly acquired staff (quickly turned-friends), we began our experiment with food.

Our partner and designer, Alex Meitlis, supplied us with a blank canvas: 'A white space with white shiny surfaces is what's going to make your concoctions stand out,' he said. We argued a little but were soon persuaded. The white background turned out to be the perfect setting for our party. And we did not intend to be shy about it.

Our food impulse

We wanted to start this book with the quip, 'If you don't like lemon or garlic… skip to the last page.' This might not be the funniest of jokes, but, considering lemon and garlic's prevalence in our recipes, it is as good a place as any to start looking for a portrait of our food. Regional descriptions just don't seem to work; there are too many influences and our food histories are long and diverse. True, we both come from a very particular part of the world – Israel/Palestine – with a unique culinary tradition. We adore the food of our childhoods. We both ate lots of fresh fruit and vegetables: oranges from Jericho, used only to make the sweetest fresh juice; crunchy little cucumbers, full of the soil's flavours; heavy pomegranates tumbling from small trees that can no longer support their weight; figs, walnuts, wild herbs… The list is endless.

We both ate a lot of street food – literally, what the name suggests. Vendors selling their produce on pavements were not restricted to 'farmers' markets'. There was nothing embarrassing or uncouth about eating on the way to somewhere. Sami remembers frequently sitting bored in front of his dinner plate, having downed a few grilled corns-on-the-cob and a couple of busbusa (coconut and semolina) cakes bought at street stalls while out with friends.

However, what makes lemon and garlic such a great metaphor for our cooking is the boldness, the zest, the strong, sometimes controversial, flavours of our childhood. The flavours and colours that shout at you, that grip you, that make everything else taste bland, pale, ordinary and insipid. Cakes drenched with rosewater-scented sugar syrup; piles of raw green almonds on ice in the market; punchy tea in a small glass with handfuls of mint and sugar; the intense smell of charred mutton cooked on an open fire; a little shop selling 20 types of crumbly ewe's and goat's milk cheeses, kept fresh in water; apricot season, when there is enough of the fruit lying around each tree to gorge yourself, the jam pot and the neighbourhood birds.

These are the sources of our impulse. It is this profusion of overwhelming sensations that inspires our desire to stun with our food, to make you say 'wow!' even if you're not the expressive type. The colours, the textures and finally the flavours that are unapologetically striking.

Our food philosophy

Like the market vendor, we make the best of what we have and don't interfere with it too much. We keep food as natural as possible, deliberately avoiding complicated cooking methods. Take our broccoli, the king of the Ottolenghi jungle. It is mightily popular (people were picketing on Ledbury Road when we tried removing it from the menu once) but it can't get any simpler. If you don't know it, you must try it (recipe on page 41); if you do, you will no doubt try it anyway.

Unfussiness and simplicity in food preparation are, for us, the only way to maintain the freshness of a dish. Each individual ingredient has a clear voice, plain characteristics that are lucid and powerful – images, tastes and aromas you remember and yearn for.

This is where we differ deeply from both complicated haute cuisine and industrial food: the fact that you can clearly taste and sense cumin or basil in our salad, that there is no room for guessing. Etti Mordo, an ex-colleague and a chef of passion, always used to say she hated dishes that you just knew had been touched a lot in the preparation.

We love real food, unadulterated and unadorned. A chocolate cake should, first and foremost, taste of chocolate. It doesn't have to involve praline, raspberries, layers of sponge, sticky liqueur and hours in the freezer. Give us a clean chocolate flavour, a muddy, fudgy texture and a plain appearance. Decorations and fancy garnishes are subject to the highs and lows of fashion. Good solid food is a source of ageless pleasure and fun.

This ability to have fun, to really enjoy food, to engage with it lightheartedly and wholeheartedly, is the key for us. After centuries of being told how bad their cuisine was, the British have started taking pride in their food in recent years, joining the European set of confident, passionate and knowledgeable devourers. Then, suddenly, they were made to feel guilty for having fun. All of a sudden it is all about diets, health, provenance, morals and food miles. Forget the food itself.

How boring, and what a mistake! This shift of focus sets us back two decades, to a time when food in the UK was just foodstuff, when it was practical instead of sensual, and so we risk once more losing our genuine pleasure in food. People will not care much about the origins of their food and how it's been grown and produced unless they first love it and are immersed in it. It is, yet again, about having fun. Don't get us wrong: supporting small farmers around the globe, treating animals humanely, making sure we don't pollute our bodies and our environment, resisting the total industrialisation of agriculture – these are all precious causes. Our wealth and the cheapness of our food give us an added responsibility to eat sensibly and ethically.

But it isn't a black-and-white choice of good versus evil when it comes to food; you can be well informed and make wise decisions about what to buy and where without turning into a fanatic. Most people's lifestyles don't allow them to grow their own vegetables or source all their meat from a local free-range farm. They must compromise without feeling guilty. So they go shopping in a supermarket during the week and visit a farmers' market at the weekend. They might choose an organic egg alongside a frozen vegetable.

This carefree but realistic approach to cooking and eating is what we try to convey with our food: the idea that cooking can be enjoyable, simple and fulfilling, yet look and taste amazing; that it mustn't be a chore or a bore, with lots of complicated ingredients to source and painstakingly prepare, but can be accessible, straightforward and frank. For us, cooking and eating are not hazy, far-off ideals but part of real life, and should be left there.

Ottolenghi

The interaction

One thing immediately evident at Ottolenghi is that you often see the chefs bringing up trays and plates heavily piled with their creations. It is a source of pride for them and for us to see a customer smile, look closely, and then gasp and give them a huge compliment. So many chefs miss out on this kind of immediate response from the diner – the reaction that leads to a leisurely chat about food.

This communication is essential to our efforts to knock down the dividing walls that characterise so many food experiences today. When was the last time you went shopping for food and actually talked to the person who made it? In a restaurant? In a supermarket? It doesn't happen. And, since cooking at home has become less common, we are deprived of this dialogue. So at Ottolenghi we are simulating a domestic food conversation in a public, urban surrounding.

The space

When you sit down to eat, it is as close as it gets to a domestic experience. The communal dining reinforces a cosy, sharing, family atmosphere. What you get is a taste of entering your mother's or grandmother's mythical kitchen, whether real or fictitious. Chefs and waiters participate, with the customer, in an intimate moment revolving around food – like a big table in the centre of a busy kitchen.

But it's not only the way you sit, it is also what surrounds you. In Ottolenghi you will always find fresh produce, the ingredients that have gone into your food, stored somewhere where you can see them. The shelves are stacked high with fruit and vegetables from the market. A half-empty box of swede might sit next to a mother with a baby in a buggy, until one of us comes upstairs and takes the vegetable down to the kitchen to cook.

The display

Once the food is on the counter, we try to limit the distance between it and the diner. We keep refrigeration to a minimum. Of course, chilling what we eat is sometimes necessary, but chilled food isn't something we'd naturally want to eat (barring ice cream and a few other exceptions). Most dishes come into their own only at room temperature or warm. It is a chemical fact. This is especially true with cakes and pastries. Their textures and flavours are destroyed beyond salvation through refrigeration.

It is a chilling experience to eat a cold sandwich, yet so many of us routinely do, and are almost oblivious to it because it is considered to be a necessary evil. With most things prepared fresh, really fresh, there is no need to chill. Every customer who comes to Ottolenghi and doesn't hear the soul-destroying hum of a brigade of stainless-steel fridges is another convert to minimal refrigeration. None of us feels much confidence in a refrigerated deli counter full of mayonnaise-based salads that might have been sitting there (in the temperature 'safe zone') for days. Conversely, it is reassuring to know that if there isn't a fridge, the salads must be fresh.

Our customers

Not many traditional hierarchies or clear-cut divisions exist in the Ottolenghi experience. You find sweet alongside savoury, hot with cold; a tray of freshly baked breads might sit next to a scrumptious array of salads, a bowl of giant meringues or a crate of tomatoes from the market. It is an air of generosity, mild chaos and lots of culinary activity that greets customers as they come in: food being presented, replaced, sold; dishes changed, trays wiped clean, the counter rearranged; lots of other people chattering and queuing.

It is this relaxed atmosphere that we strive to maintain. Casual chats with customers allow us to cater for our clients' needs. We listen and know what they like. They bring their empty dishes in for us to make them 'the best lasagne ever' (and if it's not, we will definitely hear about it). This is what encapsulates the spirit of Ottolenghi: a unique combination of quality and familiarity.

We guess that this is what drew in our first customers. So many of them have become regulars over the years, meaning not only that they come to Ottolenghi frequently but also that we recognise them, know their names and something about their lives. And vice versa. They have a favourite sales assistant who always gets their coffee just right (probably an Italian or an Aussie), their pastry of choice (Lou's rhubarb tart), their preferred seat at the table. Our close relationship with our customers extends to all of them, whether it's the bustling city stars forever on their way somewhere; the early riser eagerly tapping his watch at five-to-opening; the chilled and chatty sales assistant from next door; the eternal party organiser with a last-minute rushed order; or a mother on the look-out for something healthy to feed her and the children.

The Ottolenghi cookbook

The Ottolenghi cookbook came into existence through popular demand. So many customers asked for it that we simply had to do it. And we enjoyed every minute of it. We also loved devising recipes for our cooking classes at Leiths School of Food and Wine, some of which appear in this book. The idea of sharing our recipes with fans, as well as with a new audience, is hugely appealing. Revealing our 'secrets' is another way of interacting, of knocking down barriers, of communicating about food.

The recipes we chose for the book are a non-representative collection of old favourites, current hits and a few specials. Some of them have appeared in different guises in 'The New Vegetarian' column in the Guardian's Weekend magazine. They all represent different aspects of Ottolenghi's food – bread, the famous salads, hot dishes from the evening service in Islington, pâtisserie, cakes, cold meat and fish – and they are all typical Ottolenghi: vibrant, bold and honest.

We have decided not to include dishes incorporating long processes that have been described in detail in other, more specialised books – croissants, sourdough bread, stock. We want to stick to what is achievable at home (good croissants rarely are) and what our customers want from the cookbook. We would much rather give a couple of extra salad recipes than spend the same number of pages on chicken stock.

Introduction

My mother clearly remembers my first word, 'ma', short for marak ('soup' in Hebrew). Actually I was referring to little industrial soup croûtons, tiny yellowish pillows that she used to scatter over the tray of my highchair. I would say 'ma' when I finished them all, and point towards the dry-store cupboard.

As a small child, I loved eating. My dad, always full of expressive Italian terms, used to call me goloso, which means something like 'greedy glutton', or at least that's what I figured. I was obsessed with certain foods. I adored seafood: prawns, squid, oysters – not typical for a young Jewish lad from Jerusalem in the 1970s. A birthday treat would be to go to Sea Dolphin, a restaurant in the Arab part of the city and the only place that served non-kosher sea beasts. Their shrimps with butter and garlic were a building block of my childhood dreams.

Another vivid memory: me aged five, my brother, Yiftach, aged three. We are out on our patio, stark naked, squatting like two monkeys. We are holding pomegranates! Whenever my mom brought us pomegranates from the market, we were stripped and banished outside so we didn't stain the rug or our clothes. Trying to pick the sweet seeds clean, we still always ended up with plenty of the bitter white skin in our mouths, covered head to toe with juice.

My passion for food sometimes backfired. My German grandmother, Charlotte, once heard me say how much I loved one of her signature dishes. The result: boiled cauliflower, with a lovely coating of buttered breadcrumbs, served to me at 2 p.m. every Saturday for the next 15 years.

My other 'nonna', Luciana, never quite got over her forced exile from the family villa in Tuscany. When I think of it, she never really left. She and my nonno, Mario, created a Little Italy in a small, suburb of Tel Aviv, where they built a house with Italian furniture and fittings; they spoke Italian to the maid and a group of relatives, and ate Italian food from crockery passed down the family. Walking into their house felt like being teleported to a distant planet. There they were, my nonna and nonno, sitting in their refreshingly cool kitchen and sipping Italian coffee, nibbling the little savoury ciambelline biscuits. And then there was an unforgettable dish, unquestionably my desert-island food: gnocchi alla romana, flat semolina dumplings, grilled with butter and Parmesan.

But I started my professional life far away from the world of prawns, pomegranates and Parmesan. In my early twenties, I was a student of philosophy and literature at Tel Aviv University, a part-time teaching assistant and a budding journalist editing stories at the newsdesk of a national daily. My future with words and ideas was laid out for me in the chillingly clear colours of the inevitable – that is, a PhD.

I decided to take a little break first, an overdue gap year that was later extended into one of the longest 'years' in living memory. I came to London and, much to my poor parents' alarm, embarked on a cookery course at Le Cordon Bleu. 'Come on,' I told them, 'I just need to check this out, make sure it's not the right thing for me.'

And I wasn't so sure that it was. At 30, you are ancient in the world of catering. Being a commis-chef is plain weird. So I suffered a bit of abuse and had a few moments of teary doubt, but it became clear to me that this was the sort of creativity that suited me. I realised this when I was a pastry chef at Launceston Place, my first long-standing position in a restaurant, and one of the waiters shouted to me down the dumb-waiter shaft, 'That was the best chocolate brownie I've ever had!' I've heard this many times since.

Sami Tamimi

I was born to Palestinian parents in the old city of Jerusalem. It was a small and intimate closed society, literally existing within the ancient city walls. People could have lived their entire lives within these confines, where Muslims shared a minute space with Arab Christians and Armenians, where food was always plentiful on the street.

In a place where religion is central to so many, ours was a non-religious household. Although Arab culture and traditions were important at home, and are still very much part of my psyche, I did not have the identity that comes with a strong belief. I found it hard to know where I belonged and this was something I could not talk about at home.

From an early age I was interested in cooking and would spend many hours in the kitchen with my mother and grandmother. Cooking was the focus of daily life and formed the main part of most women's lives. Men did not cook, at least not like women did. My father, however, loved cooking for pleasure alone. My mother cooked to share the experience with her friends and the food with her family. I believe I have inherited both my father's love of food and my mother's love of feeding people.

Some of my earliest memories are of my father squatting on the floor, preparing food in the traditional Arab way. He took endless trouble over preparation, as did my mother. She would spend ages rolling perfect vine leaves, stuffed with lamb and rice, so thin and uniform they looked like green cigarettes. I remember my mother's kitchen before a wedding, when a group of friends and relatives gathered together to prepare for the event. It seemed as if there was enough food to feed the whole world!

My father was the food buyer. I only had to mention his name at the shop selling freshly roasted coffee beans and I got a bag of 'Hassan's mix'. Dad used to come home with boxes piled high with fresh fruit and vegetables. Once, when I was about seven, he arrived with a few watermelons. Being the youngest, I insisted on carrying one of them into the house, just like my brothers and sisters. On the doorstep, I couldn't hold it any longer and the massive fruit fell on the floor and exploded, covering us all with wet, red flesh.

I was 15 when I got my first job, as a kitchen porter at the Mount Zion Hotel. This is the lowliest and hardest job in any kitchen. You run around after everybody. I was lucky that the head chef saw my potential and encouraged me to cook. By then I was cooking at home all the time, making meals for my friends. I knew that this was what I wanted to do in life. It meant making the break from the Arab old city and entering Israeli life on the other side of the walls. I wanted to cook and explore the world outside, and Israeli culture allowed me to do this.

I made the significant move to Tel Aviv in 1989 and worked in various catering jobs before becoming assistant head chef at Lilith, one of the best restaurants in the city at the time. We served fresh produce, lightly cooked on a massive grill. I was entranced by this mix of Californian and Mediterranean cuisines, and it was there that I truly discovered my culinary identity and confidence. I moved to London in 1997 and was offered a job at Baker and Spice. During my six years there, I reshaped the traiteur section, introducing a variety of dishes with a strong Middle Eastern edge. This became my style. Recently I was in the kitchen looking at a box of cauliflower when my mother's cauliflower fritters came to mind, so that was what I cooked. Only then did I realise how much of my cooking is about re-creating the dishes of my childhood.

Our shared history

It was definitely some sort of providence that led us to meet for the first time in London in 1999. Our paths might have crossed plenty of times – we had had many more obvious opportunities to meet before – and yet it was only then, thousands of miles away from where we started, that we got to know each other.

We were both born in Jerusalem in 1968, Sami on the Arab east side and Yotam in the Jewish west. We grew up a few kilometres away from each other in two separate societies, forced together by a fateful war just a year earlier. Looking back now, we realise how extremely different our childhood experiences were and yet how often they converged – physically, when venturing out to the 'other side', and spiritually, sharing sensations of a place and a time.

As young gay adults, we both moved to Tel Aviv at the same time, looking for personal freedom and a sense of hope and normality that Jerusalem couldn't offer. There, we first formed meaningful relationships and took our first steps in our careers. Then, in 1997, we both arrived in London with an aspiration to broaden our horizons even further, possibly to escape again from a place we had grown out of.

So finally, on the doorstep of Baker and Spice in west London, we chatted for thirty minutes before realising that we shared a language and a history. And it was there, over the next two years, that we formed our bond of friendship and creativity.

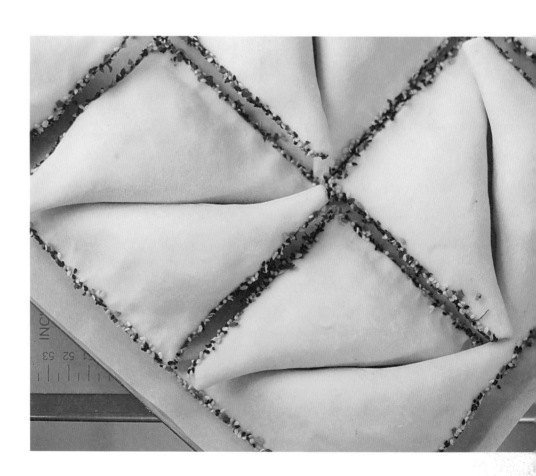

Just a few of our favourite things

We are not the type of systematically thorough chefs who are incredibly well versed in all kinds of exotic ingredients (you could easily embarrass us by naming some French cheese that we haven't got a clue about). Rather, we tend to have some star ingredients that feature over and over again, components which we love and feel at home with. These are the basic building blocks of our recipes.

Salt

We like salt and we are not embarrassed to admit it. It is vital in any dish (cakes as well) and is often underused, meaning much of your culinary effort goes to waste. We recommend salting lightly at the beginning of the cooking process and then once again, after tasting, at the end.

We use ordinary sea salt when the texture is not an issue but recommend using coarse sea salt (our favourite is Maldon) for recipes in which the salt doesn't totally dissolve during the cooking process, particularly when roasting.

Garlic

In our mind, you can't go wrong with garlic, but we are aware that some find it overwhelming, or just plain stinky. We seriously advise that you try to get hooked like us. You won't look back. Good garlic is fresh, hard and pale. Cloves that have started growing a shoot and are yellowish do not usually taste of much.

Lemon

This is another substance prone to foster addiction. Lemon juice can transform boring to exciting in a squirt.

Lemon prevents some ingredients, such as apple and avocado, from discolouring, but others, such as green beans and some fresh herbs, lose their colour soon after coming into contact with lemon juice. We often use the zest instead, which gives a wonderful aroma. Unsprayed Italian lemons with their leaves still attached are great (you can tell by the leaves how fresh they are), but they don't always have much juice.

Olive oil

We use olive oil almost everywhere, even in some cakes, where it adds moisture and a rich depth of flavour. Choose your favourite oil and keep buckets of it. For most things, we use extra virgin oil. We like the Greek Iliada. It is semi-robust with a light, grassy background aroma. For frying we'd use light olive oil or a good vegetable oil.

Fresh coriander

Although it is often associated with pastes and curries, we like to use fresh coriander in salads and light sauces. If you like the flavour, stir the leaves into roasted vegetables and wet-roasted meats and fish. It is easy and highly effective.

Mint

Alongside lemon, mint epitomises freshness. A few leaves added to a leafy salad will give it a cleansing vibrancy. Some types of mint, though, can be a little tough and bitter, so you need to chop them finely. Dried mint goes very well with yoghurt, and doesn't discolour as fresh mint does.

Yoghurt

Any Ottolenghi fan knows how obsessed we are with yoghurt. It has countless magical qualities for us. It adds an appealing lightness that counters the warmth of spicy or slow-cooked dishes. It balances and bridges contrasting flavours and textures. It lends freshness and moisture to dry ingredients. It goes well with almost anything you can think of: fresh vegetables, roasted meat and fish, hearty pulses, meringue and berries.

For most purposes we use Greek yoghurt, with up to 10 per cent fat. Because some of the liquid has been strained out, it is creamy and intense. Ordinary plain yoghurt, typically with 4 per cent fat, produces a less flavoursome sauce and you would need to use more of it to get the same result. Using low-fat yoghurt doesn't make sense at all – it is watery in texture and taste. Pure sheep's and goat's milk yoghurts are fantastically powerful.

Pomegranate and pomegranate molasses

We are not sure that we can take credit for it, but Ottolenghi started using pomegranates well before Marks & Spencer began selling little sealed punnets of the crunchy, sweet seeds, and before they won the (ever-fleeting) title of 'superfood'.

Pomegranates are easy to deseed (see Fennel and feta with pomegranate seeds and sumac on page 17) and make a fantastically attractive garnish for vegetable dishes, some roasted meat and fish and when scattered over creamy desserts. Pomegranate molasses is cooked-down pomegranate juice. It is intense, a bit like balsamic vinegar, and should be used sparingly in sauces. You can buy it from Middle Eastern grocers and some supermarkets. For buying online, try www.oilandmore.co.uk.

Tahini

Another invaluable item in our kitchen, tahini is a thick paste made from sesame seeds. We make it into a sauce (see page 272), which we add to vegetables, pulses, meat or fish, giving them sharpness and a certain richness. We don't recommend the health-shop variety of tahini, where the sesame seeds are left unhulled. It is heavy and overpowering. Use a Greek variety or a Lebanese brand, such as Al-Yaman or Al-Wadi, available from many Middle Eastern grocer's shops.

Sumac and za'atar

Sumac is a spice made from the crushed berries of a small Mediterranean tree. A dark red powder, it gives a sharp, acidic kick to salads and roasted meat.

Za'atar is a Middle Eastern blend of dried thyme, toasted sesame and salt. It is earthy, slightly tangy and used like sumac. Often the two are mixed together. Both make great garnishes for a plate of hummus or labneh (see page 272). Many supermarkets now stock sumac and za'atar with the herbs and spices. You can buy them online at www.steenbergs.co.uk or www.thespiceshop.co.uk.

Orange blossom water and rosewater

These two syrups made of blossom infusions are basic building blocks in many Mediterranean and Middle Eastern cuisines. They are used to flavour the ubiquitous baklava, as well as other cakes and desserts, and make an unusual addition to savoury dishes, mainly poultry. Use an original Lebanese brand like Cortas. You can buy them online at www.thespiceshop.co.uk.

Maple syrup

We use maple syrup to sweeten many savoury dishes. It has a substantial enough basic depth but isn't as dominant as honey. It doesn't need to dissolve, like brown sugar, so can be easily mixed into cold sauces and dressings. Hot pastries soaked with maple when just out of the oven have a glorious, warming appeal. Use pure maple syrup, nothing else.

Stock

Ideally, you'd make your own stock. Nothing beats it. You can find reliable recipes in most comprehensive cookery books (we recommend the Leiths 'bibles'). Make a large amount and freeze in small portions. Our second choice would be a bought-in real stock. Butcher's shops, delis and many supermarkets stock them. A third option is to use powder. The only one we can recommend is the Swiss organic range, Marigold. It isn't the real thing but it does (part of) the job.

Feta cheese

Moist Greek feta and similar Turkish varieties are invaluable. They enhance any vegetable, some fruits and all savoury baked products. Always look on the cheese counter before going for the vacuum-packed varieties, preferably in a Balkan or Middle Eastern deli. The unbranded chunks, swimming in murky water, are best. Ask to taste!

Sweet potatoes

This is our comfort food of choice. The astonishing thing about them is how easy they are to cook. Throw a sweet potato in the oven for up to an hour and you can scoop out the tasty, moist and (obviously) sweet flesh, ready to be scoffed on its own with a little butter, mashed, turned into a pie, added to salads, gratinated lightly, or served on the side with meat etc. Select potatoes with the ubiquitous orange flesh. The pale-fleshed ones don't do the trick.

Passion fruit

Not many ingredients taste as great as they look. Passion fruit are luscious and sensual in appearance and also have a sublime flavour. Despite their majestic qualities, they are very simple to use. Passion fruit pulp makes a most convincing sweet garnish (see the 'jam' recipe on page 276) and the juice makes a curd almost as good as lemon.

Pink peppercorns

You don't need many of these little red jewels to transform the appearance of a dish and give it a sweet, perfumed and yet not very peppery taste. We grind them in a pepper mill or with a pestle and mortar. Available online from www.steenbergs.co.uk and www.thespiceshop.co.uk.

The fear of baking

We are aware of the angst the idea of baking or making desserts evokes in some. Sorry, we are not going to try to convince you that this phobia has no grounds. Cakes and pastries can sometimes go horribly wrong, they are almost impossible to resurrect and they do take time to prepare.

Still, the gratification of good baking is unbeatable. A great tart or a bowl of homemade biscuits is a clear mark of a mature cook, and we desperately encourage any person who loves breads, cakes and sweets to try to make them at home.

Most of the recipes we selected for this book should be feasible for beginners. A few require modest baking experience. We suggest that you read through a recipe and embark on it only if you feel relatively confident. Still, we wouldn't venture on most baking recipes without some basic equipment, some of it not part of the kit of every kitchen.

Mixer

The minimum, really, is a handheld electric mixer. This will allow you to cream butter and sugar, whisk eggs and whip up creams. A much better option is a proper freestanding electric mixer, one with a whisk, a beater or paddle attachment and a dough hook. A solid brand, like Kenwood or KitchenAid, will permit you to try your hand at making brioche, breads, serious meringues and much more.

Blender

Though not essential, a blender is a very handy tool when making fruit purées and liquidising sauces and soups. The handheld stick blender is exceptionally practical, cheap and hassle-free (saves you lots of washing up).

Tins and moulds

Having the right baking tins and moulds is essential. You can make some allowances with the shape of a cake tin or a tart tin or some of their ornamental features, but essentially you need them to have certain proportions. The risks of using a shallow tin for a recipe requiring a deep one or vice versa are endless. If you have a modest collection of baking tins, you should be fine.

Palette knife and pastry brush

Small tools but absolutely essential if you want to get anywhere.

And then there are a few ingredients and techniques that are specific to the pâtisserie or bakery and need to be understood a little.

Flour

Plain flour is what we use in most of the recipes. It is relatively soft, or low in gluten, which means it will make products with a short, crumbly consistency like most cakes and biscuits. Strong flour is used to make breads and some pastries. It gives the characteristic elastic or chewy consistency. Don't substitute one type for the other when baking.

Chocolate

Unless we state otherwise, the chocolate used in our recipes should contain 52–64 per cent cocoa solids. Varieties with a higher or lower percentage would not yield the right result.

Commercial yeast

There are three main types of commercial yeast available. Fresh compressed yeast is what professional bakers use. You can find it in some healthfood shops and a few supermarkets, or if you happen to have a friendly baker in the vicinity. The best option for a home baker is dried yeast. It gives perfectly good results, is available in most supermarkets and is easy to use. Dried yeast, weight for weight, is twice as strong as fresh yeast.

The third type is fast-action dried yeast. It comes as a powder that can be added directly to the flour and does not need hydrating. It is even stronger than ordinary dried yeast. Check the instructions on the packet for the required quantity.

Creaming

This is the starting process of many cakes and biscuits, where you aerate a paste of butter and sugar before adding eggs and flour to it. It is important to incorporate as much air as the recipe specifies. The mix will go whiter and puffier the more you cream it. The eggs, afterwards, should be added a little at a time, proceeding only when the previous addition has been thoroughly incorporated into the butter and sugar. Once this is done, the dry ingredients (flour, or sometimes ground nuts) must be added all at once and you should work the mix just until everything is incorporated, no longer. You can cream with a whisk – or, better, with a beater – preferably using an electric mixer.

Greasing and lining

Brush your tins and moulds thoroughly with vegetable oil or melted butter and then line with baking parchment that has been cut to the right size. It pays off. The last thing you want is for a cake to stick obstinately to the tin.

Baking times

The issue of baking times could easily turn into a sore point after a colossal disappointment. People tend to underbake biscuits, tarts and breads and to overbake chocolate cakes and brownies. You need to keep in mind that baking times can vary a lot depending on your oven, the tin used, how full it is, and also on specific ingredients and techniques. Follow the instructions in the recipes but also try to develop an ability to observe and judge. Check well at different stages of the baking process.

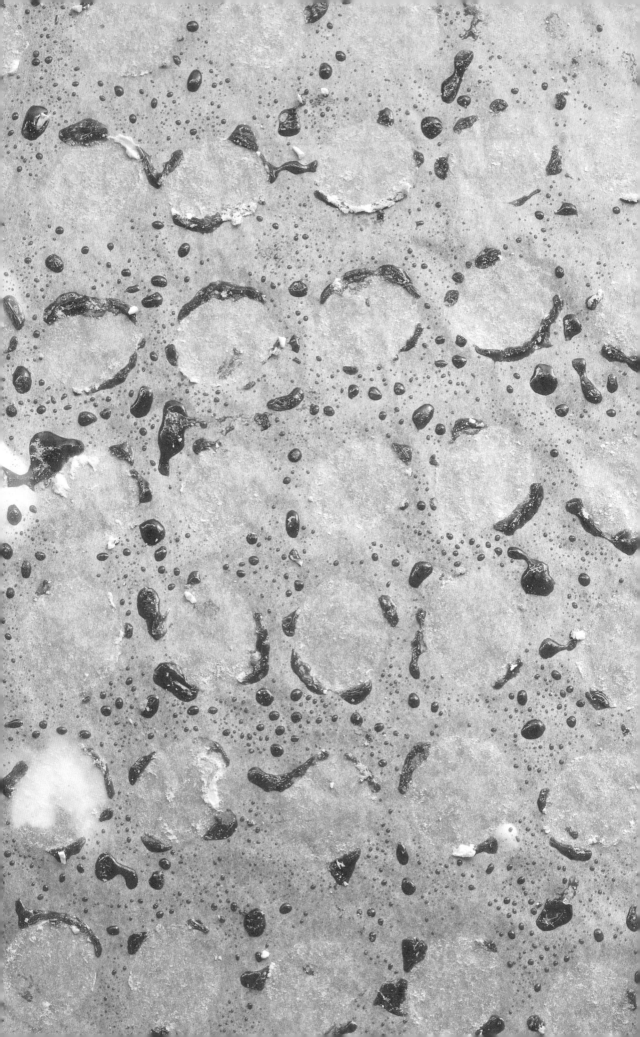

OTTOLENGHI

THE COOKBOOK

Yotam Ottolenghi and Sami Tamimi

To Ruth, Michael and Karl Yotam
To Na'ama, Hassan and Jeremy Sami

Photography by Richard Learoyd

OTTOLENGHI
THE COOKBOOK

20 19 18 17 16 15 14

Published in 2008 by Ebury Press,
an imprint of Ebury Publishing
Ebury Publishing is a division of the
Random House Group

The Random House Group Limited Reg.
No. 954009

Addresses for companies within the Random
House Group can be found at
www.randomhouse.co.uk

A CIP catalogue record for this book is available
from the British Library

The Random House Group Limited supports The
Forest Stewardship Council (FSC), the leading
international forest certification organisation. All
our titles that are printed on Greenpeace
approved FSC certified paper carry the FSC logo.
Our paper procurement policy can be found at
www.rbooks.co.uk/environment

Design and art direction: BLOK and objectif
Copy editor: Jane Middleton
Photographer: Richard Learoyd

Printed and bound in Italy by Graphicom, Srl

ISBN: 9780091922344

To buy books by your favourite authors and
register for offers visit www.rbooks.co.uk

Contents

Vegetables, pulses and grains

Chapter 1   Vegetables, pulses and grains

Chapter 1   Vegetables, pulses and grains

A substantial starter, this salad is summer bliss, offering contrasting textures and aromas. Use the best ingredients you can get your hands on – it is crucial here. Taste the peaches; they mustn't be floury, just sweet and juicy.

Yellow-fleshed peaches are normally less watery than the white variety, so they will chargrill more readily. Grilling, though, is not essential. It will add to the presentation and give a slight smokiness but you can choose to skip this stage.

Peaches and speck with orange blossom

1 Cut the peaches in half and remove the stones. Slice each half into 3 wedges, place in a bowl and add the olive oil and some salt and pepper. Toss well to coat them.
2 Place a ridged griddle pan over a high heat and leave for a few minutes so it heats up well. Place the peach wedges on the pan and grill for a minute on each side. You want to get nice charcoal lines on all sides. Remove the peaches from the pan and leave to cool.
3 Place all the dressing ingredients apart from the oil in a bowl and whisk to combine. Trickle the oil in slowly while you whisk to get a thick dressing. Season to taste.
4 On a serving platter, arrange layers of peach, endive, watercress, chard and speck. Spoon over enough dressing to coat all the ingredients but not to drench them. Serve straight away.

serves 4–6

5 ripe peaches
1 tbsp olive oil
2 red or white endives,
   leaves separated
50g watercress
50g baby chard leaves
   or other small leaves
100g speck, thinly sliced
   (10–12 slices)
coarse sea salt and black pepper

Dressing
3 tbsp orange blossom water
   ↗ page xii
1 tbsp good-quality balsamic
   vinegar
1 tbsp maple syrup
3 tbsp olive oil

This salad is a little festival in itself. The fennel and tarragon, with their echoing flavours, form a solid base on which stronger colours and flavours – pomegranate, feta, sumac – manifest themselves without overwhelming the whole salad. It is distinctly fresh and goes well with roast meats and grilled fish. Crusty bread is almost obligatory to soak up the juices from the plate.

Try substituting dried cranberries or sour cherries for the pomegranate. The fennel for this salad should be the round and bulky variety. It is crisper and sweeter than the long one.

Fennel and feta with pomegranate seeds and sumac

serves 4

½ pomegranate
2 medium fennel heads
1½ tbsp olive oil
2 tsp sumac, plus extra
  to garnish ↗ page xii
juice of 1 lemon
4 tbsp tarragon leaves
2 tbsp roughly chopped
  flat-leaf parsley
70g Greek feta cheese, sliced
salt and black pepper

1   Start by releasing the pomegranate seeds. The best way to do it is to halve the pomegranate along its 'belly' (you only need half a pomegranate here), then hold the half firmly in your hand with the seeds facing your palm. Over a large bowl, start bashing the back of the fruit with a wooden spoon. Don't hit too hard or you'll bruise the seeds and break the skin. Magically, the seeds will just fall out. Pick out any white skin that falls in.

2   Remove the leaves of the fennel, keeping a few to garnish later, and trim the base, making sure you leave enough of it still attached to hold the slices together. Slice very thinly lengthwise (a mandolin would come in handy here).

3   In a bowl, mix the olive oil, sumac, lemon juice, herbs and some salt and pepper. Add the fennel and toss well. Taste for seasoning but remember, the feta will add saltiness.

4   Layer the fennel, then the feta and then the pomegranate seeds in individual serving dishes. Garnish with fennel leaves, sprinkle over some sumac and serve immediately.

This is an ideal brunch dish for a warm spring day. With the tahini sauce and bread, it makes a modest meal in itself; without them, a colourful salad – light, refreshing and wholesome.

Here we come to the thorny issue of shelling broad beans. Many Arab recipes call for cooking and eating broad beans with their pods. This is recommended for young beans, early in the season, but wouldn't work for a fresh salad like this one. Going to the next level – skinning the beans – depends on how large the beans are, how thick their skin, and how hard you want to work. Most beans, especially the ones sold frozen, are perfectly fine eaten with the skin on. So if you prefer to skip the skinning stage, cook them for a minute longer. You'll lose a bit of the light, 'bouncy' texture but save yourself a lot of time.

Radish and broad bean salad

1   Place the broad beans in a pan of boiling water and simmer for 1–2 minutes, depending on size. Drain through a large colander and rinse in plenty of cold water to refresh them. Remove the beans from their skins by gently squeezing each one with your fingertips.

2   Cut the radishes into 6 wedges each and mix with the broad beans, onion, coriander, preserved lemon, lemon juice, parsley, olive oil and cumin. Season with salt and pepper to taste.

3   To serve, pile a mound of salad in one corner of each serving plate, pour the tahini sauce into a small bowl and stand it next to the salad. Set a pita bread next to them.

serves 4

500g shelled broad beans, fresh or frozen
350g small radishes
½ red onion, very thinly sliced
2 tbsp finely chopped coriander
30g preserved lemon, finely chopped ↗ page 273
juice of 2 lemons
2 tbsp chopped flat-leaf parsley
3 tbsp olive oil
1 tsp ground cumin
200ml Green tahini sauce ↗ page 273
4 thick pita breads
salt and black pepper

This is a recipe that is not worth making without the perfect components. Use black or green figs, or a mixture, just as long as they are ripe, sweet and heavy. Remember, figs are very illusive. Somehow, the better they look, the more tasteless they are. So see if you can sneak a taste before you buy.

The cheese we use is Pecorino Caciotta Etrusca Fresca, from Patricia Michelson of La Fromagerie. It is subtle and delicate but still has an unmistakable 'sheepy' flavour. Its soft texture complements that of the figs. A good cured ham will also work here, either instead of the cheese or in addition to it.

Figs with young pecorino and honey

serves 4 as a starter

1 Whisk together the honey and olive oil and season with salt and pepper to taste. Cut the figs into quarters. Use your hands to tear the cheese into large chunks.
2 Arrange the rocket, basil, figs and pecorino in layers on individual serving plates or a large platter. Drizzle over the honey dressing as you go along, and finish with some freshly ground black pepper.

2 tbsp good-quality honey
3 tbsp olive oil
600g ripe green or black figs
300g young pecorino or
   a similar cheese
80g rocket, preferably wild
10g basil leaves
coarse sea salt and black pepper

Our friend, Ossi Burger, says that Sami is a genius for having managed to turn something as dull as a cucumber into a delicacy in this salad. She is right about the genius thing, but that's beside the point. What Ossi has in mind is the typical mammoth cucumber that you find in supermarkets – a cucumber with no texture, no flavour and no character.

Before coming to this country, neither of us had ever come across a fresh cucumber much bigger than the typical pickled variety. Normal cucumbers, or mini cucumbers as they are sometimes called, the ones eaten in the Middle East, have a distinctive taste and are much less watery. They are earthy and crunchy throughout and can carry a whole salad without getting lost in it. The Arab bread salad, fattoush, does not work without a gutsy cucumber.

Fortunately, some organic shops and Oriental and Arab greengrocers stock these cucumbers, so always choose them if you can. If you are using a large cucumber in this salad, halve it along its centre and use a teaspoon to scoop out the seedy core, which is full of water.

Quartered radishes make a good colourful addition. Serve with other salads on a mezze plate, take with you on a picnic, or eat with roast lamb or pork.

Cucumber and poppy seed salad

serves 4

1 Chop off and discard the ends of the cucumbers. Slice the cucumbers at an angle, so you end up with pieces 1cm thick and 3–4cm long.
2 Mix together all the ingredients in a large bowl. Use your hands to massage the flavours gently into the cucumbers. Taste and adjust the amount of sugar and salt according to the quality of the cucumbers. The salad should be sharp and sweet, almost like a pickle.
3 If not serving immediately, you might need to drain some liquid off later. Adjust the seasoning again afterwards.

6 small cucumbers (about 500g)
2 mild red chillies, thinly sliced
3 tbsp roughly chopped coriander
60ml white wine vinegar or
   rice vinegar
125ml sunflower oil
2 tbsp poppy seeds
2 tbsp caster sugar
salt and black pepper

Chapter 1   Vegetables, pulses and grains

If we are totally honest, this salad is hard work. You must meticulously pick the leaves of six types of herbs, wash them carefully and then dry well. You also have to fry almonds watchfully without burning them. And you should dress it no more than a minute, literally, before serving. Quite a headache.

If you are not put off by this, however, you will find this salad one of the most gratifying dishes you can possibly make. It is astonishingly fresh, and actually makes you feel as if you are doing yourself a giant favour by eating it. Serve at the end of a substantial meal, before or instead of dessert. Otherwise, offer it alongside a hefty non-vegetarian main course. A small portion would suffice to clean the palate and make you feel a ton lighter.

This salad is the creation of Etti Mordo, the mega-talented chef who deserves lots of the credit for the creation of our Islington restaurant. A passionate perfectionist, she is one of those cooks who agonises relentlessly over a dish until she gets it just right, regardless of time and effort. Etti's food always amazes you.

Etti's herb salad

serves 6

1 Gently immerse the herb leaves in plenty of cold water, being careful not to bruise them. Drain in a colander and then dry in a salad spinner or by spreading them over a clean kitchen cloth. (Once dry, the herbs will keep in the fridge for up to one day. Store them in a sealed container lined with a few layers of kitchen paper.)
2 Heat the butter in a frying pan and add the almonds, salt and pepper. Sauté for 5–6 minutes over a low to moderate heat, until the almonds are golden. Transfer to a colander to drain. Make sure you keep the butter that's left in the pan. Leave it somewhere warm so it doesn't set. Once the almonds are cool enough to handle, chop them roughly with a large knife.
3 To assemble the salad, place the herbs in a large bowl. Add the almonds, cooking butter, lemon juice and olive oil. Toss gently and season to taste, then serve immediately.

35g coriander leaves
40g flat-leaf parsley leaves
20g dill leaves
35g tarragon leaves
30g basil leaves
40g rocket leaves
50g unsalted butter
150g whole unskinned almonds
½ tsp coarse sea salt
½ tsp black pepper
2 tbsp lemon juice
1 tbsp olive oil

As kids we used to sprinkle dried oregano over a piece of white bread covered with tomato purée and a cheap cheese, toast it and call it pizza. Fresh oregano is one of the most underused and undervalued herbs. It is potent, so must be applied with care, like rosemary or sage, but it is very versatile. It works well when added to a marinade for roasted vegetables or substantial salads. It flavours gratins and bakes and makes a great addition to green salsas for pasta, potatoes or grilled oily fish.

Marinated aubergine with tahini and oregano

serves 6 as a starter

1 Preheat the oven to 220°C/Gas Mark 7. Trim the stalk end off the aubergines, then cut each aubergine in two widthways. Cut the fat lower piece lengthways in half and then cut each half into 3 wedges. Do the same with the thinner piece but cut each half into 2 wedges. You should end up with 10 similar-sized pieces with skin on their curved side.
2 Place the aubergine pieces on a large roasting tray. Brush on all sides with plenty of olive oil and season with salt and pepper (if you want to get nice chargrill marks on the aubergines, place them on a very hot ridged griddle pan at this stage and grill for 3 minutes on each side; return them to the baking tray and continue with the next step). Place the roasting tray in the hot oven and bake the aubergines for 15–18 minutes, until they are golden brown and totally soft inside.
3 While the aubergines are roasting, make the marinade. Simply put all the ingredients in a bowl and mix well.
4 As soon as the aubergines come out of the oven, spoon the marinade over them and leave at room temperature for up to 2 hours before serving. You can store them in the fridge for up to 2 days at this stage. Make sure you don't serve them cold, though; leave them out of the fridge for an hour at least.
5 To serve, arrange the aubergines on a plate. Now, you can either spoon the tahini sauce on top and garnish with a few oregano leaves, or serve the tahini in a bowl on the side, topped with oregano leaves.

3 small aubergines
olive oil for brushing
1 quantity of Green tahini sauce
  ↗ page 272 **made without the parsley**
coarse sea salt and black pepper

Marinade
1 mild red chilli, seeded and finely chopped
2 tbsp finely chopped coriander
2 tbsp finely chopped oregano, plus a few whole leaves for garnish
1 garlic clove, crushed
3 tbsp lemon juice
4 tbsp olive oil
1 tsp coarse sea salt
¼ tsp freshly ground black pepper

To get a sublimely deep, smoky flavour from an aubergine you need to burn it. Literally. All other cooking methods pale in comparison. The messy but most effective way to do this is to burn it on a gas hob. Otherwise, you can place the aubergine under a very hot grill and allow it to cook well, until it is totally shrivelled and the skin starts to crack and flake dry.

If you go for the first choice, you will need to protect your cooker top from staining. So before starting, remove the hob heads, cover the base with aluminium foil and then place the heads back on.

This salad is Sami's mother's recipe. It is a variation on a Tunisian salad and one of our very few that doesn't contain garlic. Serve alongside other mezze salads, making sure you offer large chunks of bread with it.

Burnt aubergine with yellow pepper and red onion

serves 4

1 Place the aubergines directly on 2 separate moderate flames on the stove and roast for 12–15 minutes, turning them occasionally with metal tongs, until the flesh is soft and the skin is burnt and flaky. By this stage your kitchen will have the most magnificent charred smell. (Alternatively, place the aubergines under a hot grill for about an hour, turning them occasionally and continuing to cook even if they burst.) Leave to cool slightly.
2 Make a long cut through each warm aubergine. Using a spoon, scoop out the soft flesh while avoiding most of the burnt skin on the outside. If you don't like the seeds, try to avoid them as well. Leave the aubergine flesh to drain in a colander for at least 1 hour or overnight.
3 Chop the aubergine flesh roughly. Mix all the ingredients together, then taste and adjust the seasoning. It should be robust and pungent. Serve within 24 hours.

2 medium aubergines
2 yellow or green peppers,
  cored and cut into 1.5cm dice
1 medium red onion,
  roughly chopped
24 cherry tomatoes, halved
40g flat-leaf parsley,
  roughly chopped
70ml sunflower or nut oil
90ml cider vinegar
3 tsp ground cumin
coarse sea salt and black pepper

This dish, one of Ramael Scully's, makes a superb warm vegetarian starter or main course. Scully, as he is known to everyone, is our evening chef in Islington, and serves complex dishes of outstanding quality without ever losing his cool.

You need to start this recipe at least four hours in advance, preferably the night before, for the gnocchi mix to rest properly. The quality of the ricotta is paramount.

Aubergine-wrapped ricotta gnocchi with sage butter

serves 4 as a starter, 2 as a main course

1 small to medium aubergine
4 tbsp olive oil
20g unsalted butter, melted
15g Parmesan cheese, freshly grated

Ricotta gnocchi
30g pine nuts
250g ricotta cheese
2 free-range egg yolks
35g plain flour
40g Parmesan cheese, freshly grated
1 tbsp chopped flat-leaf parsley
1 tbsp chopped basil
¼ tsp grated nutmeg
½ tsp salt
a good grinding of black pepper

Sage butter
90g unsalted butter
20 sage leaves
a pinch of salt
½ tbsp lemon juice (optional)

1 Place the pine nuts in a small frying pan and dry-roast over a medium heat for 3–4 minutes, stirring them occasionally so they colour evenly. Transfer to a large bowl and add the ricotta, egg yolks, flour, grated Parmesan, herbs, nutmeg, salt and pepper. Stir well, then cover and refrigerate for 4 hours or overnight.

2 Preheat the oven to 180°C/Gas Mark 4. Trim the top and bottom off the aubergine and cut it lengthways into 5mm-thick slices; you will need 8–12 slices, depending on how many gnocchi you make. Lay the slices on a baking tray lined with baking parchment and brush liberally with the olive oil. Place in the oven and roast for 10–15 minutes, until tender and golden (alternatively, you could chargrill the aubergine slices over a medium heat for 2–3 minutes on each side).

3 To shape the gnocchi, wet your hands and scoop out 40–50g portions (about 3 tablespoons). Roll into 8 or 12 elongated barrel shapes. Meanwhile, bring plenty of salted water to the boil in a large saucepan.

4 Carefully add a few dumplings to the simmering water – don't cook them all at once or they will stick to each other. After about 2 minutes, they should rise to the surface. Using a slotted spoon, transfer them to a tea towel to drain. Pat dry with kitchen paper and brush them with the melted butter.

5 Once the gnocchi have cooled down, take a strip of aubergine and wrap it around the centre of each one, like a belt. Trim the aubergine so that the seam is at the bottom. Place the gnocchi in a greased ovenproof dish and set aside. You can cover them with cling film and keep them in the fridge for a day at this stage.

6 When ready to serve, sprinkle the gnocchi with the Parmesan and bake in the oven at 180°C/Gas Mark 4 for 8–10 minutes, until they are heated through.

7 Meanwhile, quickly make the sage butter sauce, as it needs to coincide with the gnocchi. Place a small saucepan over a moderate heat. Add the butter and allow it to simmer for a few minutes until it turns a light golden-brown colour and has a nutty smell. Remove from the heat and carefully add the sage, salt and lemon juice, if using. Return to the heat for a few seconds to cook the sage lightly.

8 Divide the gnocchi between serving plates, pour the hot butter on top with a few sage leaves and serve immediately.

This is probably the archetypal Ottolenghi salad: robust contrasting flavours, vibrant and vivacious colours, fresh herbs and nuts – laid out generously to reveal all of the dish's elements.

To create the most impact, we recommend that you serve it from a communal plate brought out to the dining table. It makes an exciting starter and doesn't need much else beside it.

Roasted aubergine with saffron yoghurt

1 For the sauce, infuse the saffron in the hot water in a small bowl for 5 minutes. Pour the infusion into a bowl containing the yoghurt, garlic, lemon juice, olive oil and some salt. Whisk well to get a smooth, golden sauce. Taste and adjust the salt, if necessary, then chill. This sauce will keep well in the fridge for up to 3 days.

2 Preheat the oven to 220°C/Gas Mark 7. Place the aubergine slices on a roasting tray, brush with plenty of olive oil on both sides and sprinkle with salt and pepper. Roast for 20–35 minutes, until the slices take on a beautiful light brown colour. Let them cool down. The aubergines will keep in the fridge for 3 days; just let them come to room temperature before serving.

3 To serve, arrange the aubergine slices on a large plate, slightly overlapping. Drizzle the saffron yoghurt over them, sprinkle with the pine nuts and pomegranate seeds and lay the basil on top.

serves 4

3 medium aubergines,
 cut into slices 2cm thick, or into
 wedges ↗ page 26
olive oil for brushing
2 tbsp toasted pine nuts
a handful of pomegranate seeds
20 basil leaves
coarse sea salt and black pepper

Saffron yoghurt
a small pinch of saffron strands
3 tbsp hot water
180g Greek yoghurt
1 garlic clove, crushed
2½ tbsp lemon juice
3 tbsp olive oil

- Selection of
  - small box
  - large box

- main sold

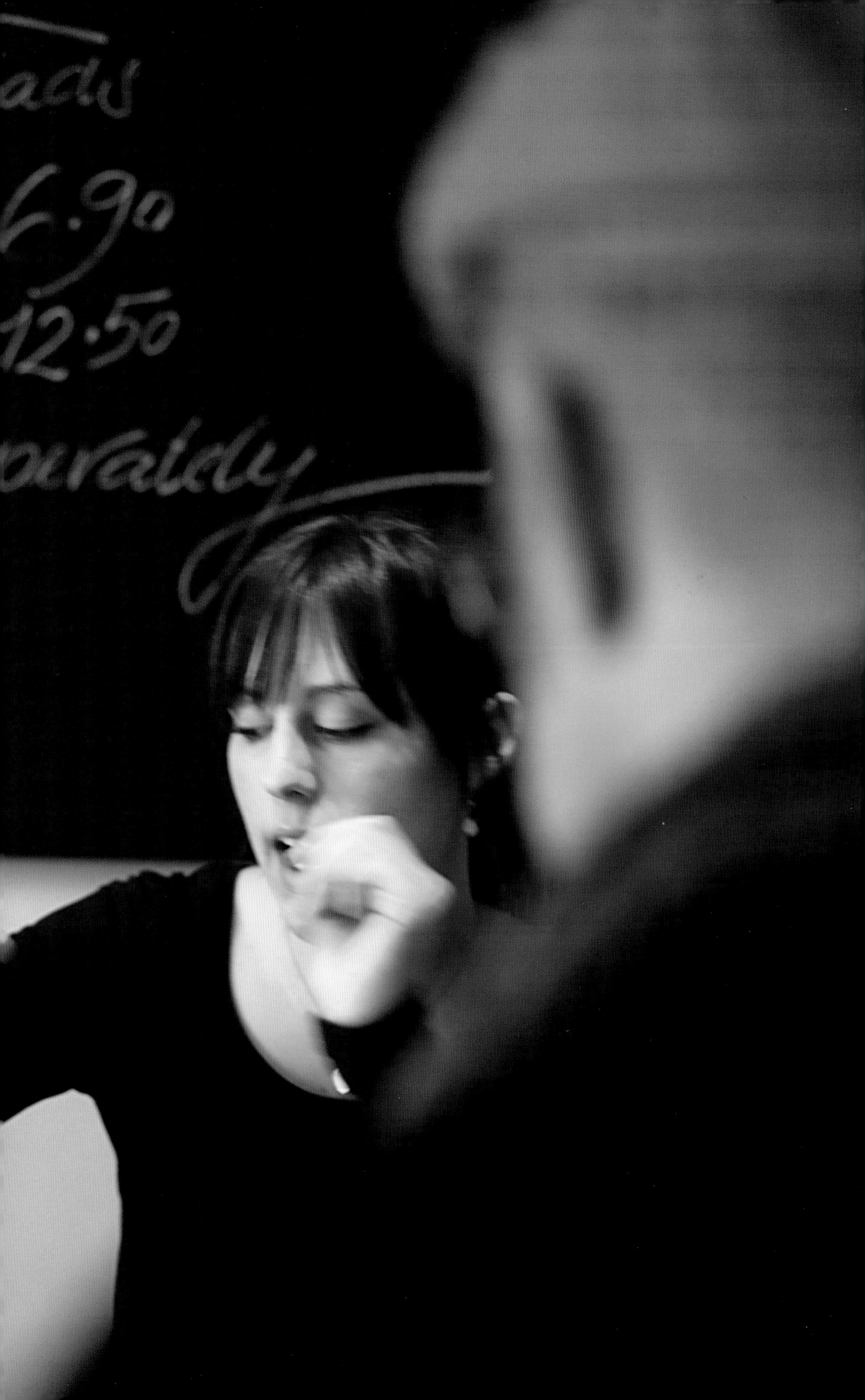
6.90
12.50

Chapter 1 Vegetables, pulses and grains

This generous salad is almost a meal in itself. It is laden with enough colours, textures and aromas to be the centre of a light spring supper. Its generous creator is Helen Goh, with whom we have had the pleasure of working for the past two years. Since arriving from Australia, Helen has been a continuous source of inspiration and insight for everybody at Ottolenghi, both as a chef and as a sensitive friend.

Manouri is a Greek semi-soft fresh cheese produced from the drained whey left over after making feta. It is light and creamy and we love using it for its subtlety and the fact that it fries well and keeps its shape. If you can't get hold of it, use a light goat's cheese such as Rosary, but skip the frying as it will disintegrate. If you like haloumi, it fries and grills very well and will also work here.

Chargrilled asparagus, courgettes and manouri

serves 4–6

1 There is a fair amount of vegetable preparation here before making the basil oil and assembling the salad. Start with the tomatoes. Preheat the oven to 170°C/Gas Mark 3. Mix the tomatoes with 3 tablespoons of the olive oil and season with some salt and pepper. Spread them out on a baking tray lined with baking parchment, skin side down. Roast in the oven for 50 minutes or until semi-dried. You can leave them there a bit more or a bit less, depending on how dry you like them. They will be delicious anyway. Remove from the oven and leave to cool.

2 Trim the woody bases of the asparagus and blanch for 4 minutes in plenty of boiling water. Drain and refresh under cold water, making sure the spears are completely cold. Drain well again, then transfer to a mixing bowl and toss with 2 tablespoons of the remaining olive oil and some salt and pepper.

3 Slice the courgettes very thinly lengthwise, using a mandolin (this inexpensive tool will make your kitchen life dramatically easier) or a vegetable peeler. Mix with 1 tablespoon of the olive oil and some salt and pepper.

4 Place a ridged griddle pan on a high heat and leave there for a few minutes. It should be very hot. Grill the courgettes and asparagus, turning them over after about a minute. You want to get nice char marks on all sides. Remove and leave to cool.

5 Heat the remaining 3 tablespoons of olive oil in a pan. Fry the manouri cheese for 3 minutes on each side or until it is golden. Place on kitchen paper to soak up the excess oil. Alternatively, chargrill the cheese on the hot griddle pan for about 2 minutes on each side.

6 To make the basil oil, blitz all the ingredients in a blender until smooth. You might need to double the quantity for some blender blades to be effective. Keep any extra oil for future salads.

7 To assemble, arrange the rocket, vegetables and cheese in layers on a flat serving plate. Try to build the salad up whilst showing all the individual components. Drizzle with as much basil oil as you like and serve.

350g cherry tomatoes, halved
140ml olive oil
24 asparagus spears
2 courgettes
200g manouri cheese, sliced
   2cm thick
25g rocket
coarse sea salt and black pepper

Basil oil
75ml olive oil
1 garlic clove, chopped
25g basil leaves
a pinch of salt
¼ tsp black pepper

Salty, tender and juicy, samphire grows on tidal stretches of the British coast from June to September. It can be a challenge to get your hands on, especially at both ends of the season, but we highly recommend nagging your fishmonger for some. It adds the flavour of the sea to fish and salads in the same way that seaweed does, but has a unique, succulent texture. Here we combine 'poor man's asparagus', as it is sometimes referred to, with its rich counterpart to create an attractive salad, full of flavours and many shades of green. Serve as an accompaniment to fried fish or on its own as a starter.

Asparagus and samphire

serves 4

1 tbsp black sesame seeds
   (if not available, use white ones)
24 medium-thick asparagus spears
100g samphire, washed
2 tbsp olive oil
1 tbsp sesame oil
1 garlic clove, crushed
2 tbsp picked tarragon leaves
coarse sea salt and black pepper

1 Put the sesame seeds in a non-stick pan and place over a medium heat for 2–3 minutes, just to toast them gently. Remove from the heat and set aside.
2 To cook the greens, fill a large saucepan with plenty of cold water and bring to the boil. You don't need to add salt; samphire is salty enough. Trim the woody bases of the asparagus and put the spears in the boiling water. Blanch for 2–3 minutes, then add the samphire. Cook for another minute, until the asparagus is tender but still firm.
3 Drain the greens in a large colander and run lots of cold water over them. It's very important to get them completely cold. Leave in the colander to drain and then dry with a kitchen towel.
4 To finish the salad, put the asparagus and samphire in a bowl and mix with the rest of the ingredients. Toss well, then taste and adjust the seasoning. You might not need any extra salt. Serve straight away, or chill and serve within 24 hours.

Green beans are so popular at Ottolenghi that we seem to be constantly
on the lookout for new combinations. Orange and hazelnut go wonderfully
well together. They offer a good balance of freshness and earthiness
and the flavours are subtle enough to complement the beans without
overpowering them.

The beans can be cooked and chilled a day in advance and then
dressed before serving. Sugarsnaps, green peas and broad beans can
substitute any of the other two beans or be added to the salad.

French beans and mangetout
with hazelnut and orange

serves 6

400g French beans
400g mangetout
70g unskinned hazelnuts
1 orange
20g chives, roughly chopped
1 garlic clove, crushed
3 tbsp olive oil
2 tbsp hazelnut oil
 (or another nut oil, if unavailable)
coarse sea salt and black pepper

1 Preheat the oven to 180°C/Gas Mark 4. Using a small, sharp knife,
   trim the stalk ends off the French beans and the mangetout, keeping
   the two separate. Bring plenty of unsalted water to the boil in a large
   saucepan – you need lots of space for the beans, as this is crucial
   for preserving their colour. Blanch the French beans in the water for
   4 minutes, then drain into a colander and run them under plenty of
   tap water until cold. Leave to drain and dry. Repeat with the
   mangetout, but blanch for only 1 minute.
2 While the beans are cooking, scatter the hazelnuts over a baking
   tray and roast in the oven for 10 minutes. Leave until cool enough
   to handle, then rub them in a clean tea-towel to get rid of most of the
   skin. Chop the nuts with a large, sharp knife. They should be quite
   rough; some can even stay whole.
3 Using a vegetable peeler, remove the zest from the orange in strips,
   being careful to avoid the bitter white pith. Slice each piece of zest
   into very thin strips (if you have a citrus zester, you could do the
   whole job with that).
4 To assemble the dish, mix all the ingredients together in a bowl,
   toss gently, then taste and adjust the seasoning. Serve at room
   temperature.

This combination is a manifestation of spring. The pink peppercorns add a sweet, scented aroma to the freshness of the vegetables.

Claudia Roden, the godmother of Middle Eastern cookery and a venerable inspiration for us, has a similar recipe. She suggests using frozen artichoke bottoms and broad beans as alternatives to fresh. If she can do it, so can you. This will definitely save you lots of time without paying a huge price in terms of flavour.

Serve this dish at room temperature. It makes a fine starter served with hearty bread. You can chill it and keep in the fridge for up to one day.

Baked artichokes and broad beans

serves 2–4

1   Preheat the oven to 200°C/Gas Mark 6. Juice the lemons and discard all but 2 of the empty lemon halves.
2   To clean the artichokes, cut off most of the stalk and start removing the tough outer leaves by hand. Once you reach the softer leaves, take a sharp serrated knife and trim off 1–2cm from the top of the artichoke. Cut the artichoke in half lengthways so you can reach the heart and scrape it clean. Use a small, sharp knife to remove all the 'hairs'. Immediately rub the heart with a little lemon juice to prevent it discolouring. Cut each artichoke half into slices 5mm thick. Place in cold water and stir in half the remaining lemon juice.
3   Drain the artichoke slices and spread them out on a baking tray. Add the remaining lemon juice, the 2 reserved lemon halves and all the rest of the ingredients except the broad beans, peas and parsley. Cover with foil and bake for 45–60 minutes or until the artichokes are tender. Remove from the oven, take off the foil and let the artichokes cool down.
4   Fill a large saucepan with plenty of cold water and bring to the boil. Add the broad beans and peas and blanch for 2 minutes, then drain in a colander and run under cold water to refresh. Leave in the colander to dry. If the broad beans are large and have tough skins, you may want to remove them. Simply press each one gently with your fingertips until the bean pops out.
5   Remove the lemon halves from the artichokes. Mix the artichokes with the beans, peas and parsley, and stir in the lemon slices. Taste for salt and pepper, plate, sprinkle with peppercorns and serve.

4 lemons, plus a few thin lemon slices to finish
2 large globe artichokes
2 bay leaves
2 sprigs of thyme
2 garlic cloves, thinly sliced
1 tbsp pink peppercorns, plus extra to garnish ↗ page xiv
125ml white wine
60ml olive oil
250g shelled broad beans
250g shelled peas
1 bunch of flat-leaf parsley, roughly chopped
salt and black pepper

This is another of Helen's contributions, bringing an Oriental brushstroke to the generally Mediterranean Ottolenghi canvas. Served at room temperature, it is soothingly sweet and goes well with roast chicken or beef.

Broccolini, or tender-stem broccoli, is a hybrid between broccoli and Chinese kale (gai lan). Cooked very lightly, it has a great tender bite.

Use kecap manis (sweet soy sauce), if you can get hold of it. Otherwise use a standard variety. For the chilli sauce, choose one that is not too sweet. Reduce the quantity if it is very hot.

Sweet broccolini with tofu, sesame and coriander

serves 4

3 tbsp kecap manis (sweet soy sauce)
4 tbsp chilli sauce or paste
2 tbsp sesame oil
250g firm tofu *(tau kwa)*
450g broccolini
1 tbsp sesame seeds
1 tbsp groundnut oil
3 tbsp coriander leaves

1 First, marinate the tofu. In a bowl, whisk the soy sauce, chilli sauce and sesame oil together. Cut the tofu into strips about 1cm thick, mix gently (so it doesn't break) with the marinade and leave in the fridge for half an hour.

2 Trim any hard leaves off the broccolini and discard. Place the broccolini in a large saucepan full of boiling water and blanch for 2 minutes. Drain in a colander and run at once under a cold tap to stop further cooking. Leave to dry.

3 Scatter the sesame seeds in a non-stick pan and place it over a medium heat for about 5 minutes. Jiggle them around so they toast evenly and then remove from the heat.

4 Place a wok or a thick iron pan over a high heat and allow it to heat up well. Add the groundnut oil. Reduce the heat to medium to prevent the oil spitting (it may spit a little), then carefully add the tofu strips and leave for 2–3 minutes, until they colour underneath. Using tongs, gently turn them over to colour the other side. (If you are making a large quantity, you may need to fry the tofu in 2 or 3 batches, otherwise it will 'stew' rather than fry.)

5 Add any remaining marinade to the pan, plus the cooked broccolini. Add the coriander and half the sesame seeds and stir together gently. Remove from the heat and let everything come to room temperature in the pan. Taste and add more sesame oil, soy sauce or salt if necessary. Divide between serving plates and sprinkle with the remaining sesame seeds.

If there's a dish that's become synonymous with Ottolenghi, second only to our meringues, it is this one. Customers come especially for it and always complain that their broccoli is never as exciting as ours. In all honesty, broccoli is a boring vegetable and you do need a magic touch to bring it to life.

If followed carefully, this recipe does the trick. It has a bit of a history in itself. Sami started cooking it at Baker and Spice after having brought it over from Lilith, a restaurant in Tel Aviv. It is still a winner at Baker and Spice and at Ottolenghi, even though standard broccoli is losing popularity to the tender purple sprouting broccoli.

For even more oomph, add four chopped anchovy fillets to the chilli and garlic when cooking them in the oil.

Chargrilled broccoli with chilli and garlic

serves 2–4

2 heads of broccoli (about 500g)
115ml olive oil
4 garlic cloves, thinly sliced
2 mild red chillies, thinly sliced
coarse sea salt and black pepper
toasted flaked almonds or very
   thin slices of lemon (with skin),
   to garnish (optional)

1 Prepare the broccoli by separating it into florets (leave on the individual small stems that the florets grow on). Fill a large saucepan with plenty of water and bring to the boil. It should be big enough to accommodate the broccoli easily. Throw in the broccoli and blanch for 2 minutes only. Don't be tempted to cook it any longer! Using a large slotted spoon, quickly transfer the broccoli to a bowl full of ice-cold water – you need to stop the cooking at once. Drain in a colander and allow to dry completely. It is important that the broccoli isn't wet at all. In a mixing bowl, toss the broccoli with 45ml of the olive oil and a generous amount of salt and pepper.

2 Place a ridged griddle pan over a high heat and leave it there for at least 5 minutes, until it is extremely hot. Depending on the size of your pan, grill the broccoli in several batches. The florets mustn't be cramped. Turn them around as they grill so they get char marks all over. Transfer to a heatproof bowl and continue with another batch.

3 While grilling the broccoli, place the rest of the oil in a small saucepan with the garlic and chillies. Cook them over a medium heat until the garlic just begins to turn golden brown. Be careful not to let the garlic and chilli burn – remember, they will keep on cooking even when off the heat. Pour the oil, garlic and chilli over the hot broccoli and toss together well. Taste and adjust the seasoning.

4 Serve warm or at room temperature. You can garnish the broccoli with almonds or lemon just before serving, if you like.

This hearty combination of flavours makes an impressive vegetarian starter. It is assembled at the last minute and served warm.

Salsify is a long root that can be hard to find but is worth the effort for its delicate, earthy flavour. Good substitutes would be celeriac or Jerusalem artichokes. Purple sprouting broccoli is available in late winter and early spring. The stems can be quite woody and will need trimming down from the excess leaves (Helen uses the leaves in a delicious dish of shiitake mushrooms and oyster sauce). If the stems are thick, cut them lengthways into 2 or 4 so they are the same thickness as an asparagus spear. Broccolini (↗ page 39) can be substituted for the purple sprouts.

Purple sprouting broccoli and salsify with caper butter

serves 4 as a starter

juice of 2½ lemons
4 salsify (or scorzonera) roots
400g trimmed purple sprouting broccoli (about 600g before trimming)
100g cold unsalted butter
2 tbsp baby capers, drained
2 tbsp finely chopped chives
2 tbsp finely chopped flat-leaf parsley
2 tbsp finely chopped tarragon
2 tbsp roughly chopped dill
salt and pepper

1 Bring a pan of salted water to the boil with 2 tablespoons of the lemon juice. Peel the salsify and cut each one into 3 batons. Add to the boiling water and simmer for 10 minutes or until al dente. Remove from the water with a slotted spoon and allow to cool a little. Cut each baton in half lengthwise and then the same way again.
2 Simmer the broccoli in the same water for 3 minutes, until slightly tenderised, then drain and keep warm. (You can stop at this stage and do the rest just before serving; if you choose to do this, you will need to refresh the broccoli under cold water after draining and then reheat it before serving by quickly tossing it with a little oil in a small pan.)
3 Heat half the butter in a frying pan over medium heat. When it is foaming, add the salsify and fry until golden brown. Season with salt and pepper, then remove from the pan and arrange on serving plates with the broccoli. Give it height by shaping it like a pyramid. Keep in a warm place.
4 To make the caper butter sauce, reheat the frying pan until nearly smoking. Throw in the remaining butter and cook it from gold to a nut brown. Be brave! When you reach the right colour, take the pan off the heat and gently pour in the remaining lemon juice. Be careful, it will spit. Throw in the capers and herbs and season well.
5 Immediately pour the caper butter over the arranged vegetables and serve.

You either love it or hate it? Not totally so. This okra dish should convert some stubborn okra haters. Okra can be slimy but here that is minimised by removing the stalks carefully, without exposing the gloopy seeds, and by baking the okra whole rather than stewing it. The gingery sauce is light and clean.

Baked okra with tomato and ginger

serves 2–4

1 Preheat the oven to 200°C/Gas Mark 6. To prepare the okra, take a small, sharp knife and carefully remove the stalk end. Try not to cut very low; leave the end of the stalk to seal the main body of the fruit, so the seeds are not exposed.

2 Mix the okra with 3 tablespoons of the olive oil and some salt and pepper. Scatter in a roasting tray in a single layer, then place in the oven and bake for 15–20 minutes, until just tender.

3 Meanwhile, prepare the sauce. Heat the remaining oil in a large saucepan, add the garlic, ginger and chilli flakes and fry for about a minute. Add the tomatoes, sugar and some salt and pepper and cook, uncovered, over a medium heat for 10 minutes, until the mixture thickens slightly.

4 When the okra is ready, stir it gently into the sauce and cook for 2 minutes. To serve warm, spoon the okra on to serving plates and scatter the coriander on top. If serving at room temperature, adjust the seasoning again before serving and garnish with the coriander.

500g okra
5 tbsp olive oil
2 garlic cloves, crushed
1 knob of fresh ginger (about 12g), finely chopped
¼ tsp dried chilli flakes
3 large ripe tomatoes, finely chopped
2 tsp caster sugar
1½ tbsp coriander leaves
salt and pepper

Butternut squash has softer skin than other pumpkins and is therefore easier to prepare. For us it is almost a staple.

Butternut's mild sweetness and firm flesh make it suitable to go alongside most main courses, but also to serve on its own as a vegetarian centrepiece.

Roasted butternut squash with burnt aubergine and pomegranate molasses

serves 2–4

1 Preheat the oven to 220°C/Gas Mark 7. Trim the top and bottom off the butternut squash and cut it in half lengthways. Remove the seeds using a small knife or a spoon. Cut each half into wedges 2–3cm thick. Arrange the wedges in a roasting tray, standing them up with the skin underneath if possible. Brush with half the olive oil and season generously with salt and pepper. Place in the oven for 25–30 minutes, by which time the wedges should be tender and slightly browned. Leave to cool.

2 Reduce the oven temperature to 180°C/Gas Mark 4. Scatter the seeds and almonds on a roasting tray and toast for 8–10 minutes, until lightly browned. Leave to cool.

3 For the sauce, place the aubergine directly on a moderate flame on a gas hob (you might want to cover the hob top with foil before you begin ↗ page 27). Burn the aubergine for 12–15 minutes, until the skin dries and cracks and smoky aromas are released. Turn it around occasionally, using metal tongs. Remove from the heat and leave to cool slightly. (Alternatively, you can place the aubergine under a very hot grill for about an hour, turning it around occasionally; continue until well shrivelled on the outside, even if it bursts.)

4 Make a long cut through the aubergine. Using a spoon, scoop out the soft flesh while avoiding most of the burnt skin. Drain in a colander for 10 minutes, then transfer to a board and chop roughly.

5 In a mixing bowl stir together the aubergine flesh, yoghurt, oil, pomegranate molasses, lemon juice, parsley and garlic. Taste and season with salt and pepper. It should be sweetly sharp and highly flavoursome.

6 Arrange the squash wedges on a serving platter, piling them up on top of each other. Drizzle with the remaining olive oil, sprinkle the nuts and seeds over and garnish with the basil. Serve the sauce on the side.

1 large butternut squash
4 tbsp olive oil
1 tbsp pumpkin seeds
1 tbsp sunflower seeds
1 tbsp black sesame seeds
  (if unavailable, use white ones)
1 tsp nigella seeds
10g sliced almonds
10g basil leaves
coarse sea salt and black pepper

Sauce
1 medium aubergine
150g Greek yoghurt, at room
  temperature
2 tbsp olive oil
1½ tsp pomegranate molasses
  ↗ page xii
3 tbsp lemon juice
1 tbsp coarsely chopped
  flat-leaf parsley
1 garlic clove, crushed

Nir Feller, who's got the most infectious zeal for food, helped develop this dish when running our kitchen in Notting Hill. It is ideal for preparing ahead of time. Have it ready in the baking dish and put it in the oven just when you need it. It makes an impressive starter for a cold winter night.

Caramelised endive with Serrano ham

serves 6

1 Preheat the oven to 200°C/Gas Mark 6. Begin by caramelising the endive. You will probably have to do it in 2–3 batches, depending on the size of your largest frying pan; the endive halves need to fit lying flat without overlapping. If working in 2 batches, put half the butter and half the sugar in the pan and place over a high heat. Stir to mix. As soon as the butter starts to bubble, place 6 endive halves facing down in the pan and fry for 2–3 minutes, until golden. You might need to press them down slightly. Don't worry if the butter goes slightly brown. Remove and repeat the process with the remaining butter, sugar and 6 endive halves.

2 Line a tray with baking parchment and arrange the endives on it, caramelised side facing up. Sprinkle with a little salt and pepper.

3 Mix the breadcrumbs, Parmesan, thyme, cream, ¼ teaspoon salt and a good grind of black pepper. Spoon this mixture over the endives and top each one with a slice of ham. Roast in the oven for 15–20 minutes, until the endives feel soft when poked with a knife. Serve hot or warm, drizzled with some olive oil and sprinkled with the chopped parsley, if using.

6 endives, cut in half lengthways
40g unsalted butter
4 tsp caster sugar
50g sourdough breadcrumbs
70g Parmesan cheese, freshly grated
2 tbsp thyme leaves
120ml whipping cream
12 thin slices of Serrano ham
olive oil for drizzling
2 tsp chopped flat-leaf parsley (optional)
coarse sea salt and black pepper

These addictive fritters are Sami's mother's recipe. She used to make them once a week and give them to the kids in a pita to take to school for lunch. They are not dissimilar to Indian pakoras. Best eaten hot or warm or taken on a picnic – in a pita, of course, with some hummus and tomato.

Cauliflower and cumin fritters with lime yoghurt

serves 4

1 Put all the sauce ingredients in a bowl and whisk well. Taste – looking for a vibrant, tart, citrusy flavour – and adjust the seasoning. Chill or leave out for up to an hour.
2 To prepare the cauliflower, trim off any leaves and use a small knife to divide the cauliflower into little florets. Add them to a large pan of boiling salted water and simmer for 15 minutes or until very soft. Drain into a colander.
3 While the cauliflower is cooking, put the flour, chopped parsley, garlic, shallots, eggs, spices, salt and pepper in a bowl and whisk together well to make a batter. When the mixture is smooth and homogenous, add the warm cauliflower. Mix to break down the cauliflower into the batter.
4 Pour the sunflower oil into a wide pan to a depth of 1.5cm and heat up. When it is very hot, carefully spoon in generous portions of the cauliflower mixture, 3 tablespoons per fritter. Take care with the hot oil! Space the fritters apart with a fish slice, making sure they are not overcrowded. Fry in small batches, controlling the oil temperature so the fritters cook but don't burn. They should take 3–4 minutes on each side.
5 Remove from the pan and drain well on a few layers of kitchen paper. Serve with the sauce on the side.

1 small cauliflower (about 320g)
120g plain flour
3 tbsp chopped flat-leaf parsley, plus a few extra leaves to garnish
1 garlic clove, crushed
2 shallots, finely chopped
4 free-range eggs
1½ tsp ground cumin
1 tsp ground cinnamon
½ tsp ground turmeric
1½ tsp salt
1 tsp black pepper
500ml sunflower oil for frying

Lime sauce
300g Greek yoghurt
2 tbsp finely chopped coriander
grated zest of 1 lime
2 tbsp lime juice
2 tbsp olive oil
salt and pepper

Like broccoli, cauliflower can be rather dull. So here we give it the classic Ottolenghi treatment of chargrilling and then drenching with vigorous flavours while still hot. The combination of ingredients in this recipe might sound unusual but it works wonderfully well. Try it with a plain roast chicken.

Chargrilled cauliflower with tomato, dill and capers

serves 2–4

1 First make the dressing, either by hand or in a food processor. Mix together the capers, mustard, garlic, vinegar and some salt and pepper. Whisk vigorously or run the machine while adding half the oil in a slow trickle. You should get a thick, creamy dressing. Taste and adjust the seasoning.
2 Add the cauliflower florets to a large pan of boiling salted water and simmer for 3 minutes only. Drain through a colander and run under a cold tap to stop the cooking immediately. Leave in the colander to dry well. Once dry, place in a mixing bowl with the remaining olive oil and some salt and pepper. Toss well.
3 Place a ridged griddle pan over the highest possible heat and leave it for 5 minutes or until very hot. Grill the cauliflower in a few batches – make sure the florets are not cramped. Turn them around as they grill, then once nicely charred, transfer to a bowl. While the cauliflower is still hot, add the dressing, dill, spinach and tomatoes. Stir together well, then taste and adjust the seasoning.
4 Serve warm or at room temperature, adjusting the seasoning again at the last minute.

2 tbsp capers, drained and roughly chopped
1 tbsp French wholegrain mustard
2 garlic cloves, crushed
2 tbsp cider vinegar
120ml olive oil
1 small cauliflower, divided into florets
1 tbsp chopped dill
50g baby spinach leaves
20 cherry tomatoes, halved
coarse sea salt and black pepper

Chapter 1 Vegetables, pulses and grains

Considering the colossal amounts of food coming out of our kitchen in Notting Hill, visitors are always astonished to see how small it is. Sharing such small quarters can lead to extraordinary kinds of personal interaction, with the occasional tense moment between the savoury chefs and the pastry department.

On a culinary level, this yields some unusual hybrids. Using the pastry department's crumble mix for this gratin was originally Sami's revenge for some freshly squeezed lemon juice that was 'stolen' by a pastry chef to make curd. It turned out that the creamy sweetness of the crumble offsets the dominant savoury tones of the fennel and the acidity of the tomato to create a most comforting experience.

You can have this ready well in advance and put it in the oven at the last minute.

Fennel, cherry tomato and crumble gratin

serves 6–8

1 Preheat the oven to 200°C/Gas Mark 6. Trim off the fennel stalks and cut each bulb lengthways in half. Cut each half into slices 1.5cm thick. Place in a large bowl with the olive oil, thyme leaves, garlic, salt and pepper and toss together. Transfer to an ovenproof dish and pour the cream over the fennel. Mix the crumble with the grated Parmesan and scatter evenly on top.
2 Cover the dish with foil and bake for 45 minutes. Remove the foil and arrange the tomatoes on top. You can leave some on the vine and scatter some loose. Scatter a few thyme sprigs on top. Return to the oven and bake for another 15 minutes. By now the fennel should feel soft when poked with a knife and the gratin should have a nice golden colour. Remove from the oven and allow to rest for a few minutes. Sprinkle chopped parsley over and serve hot or warm.

1kg fennel bulbs
3 tbsp olive oil
1 tbsp thyme leaves, plus a few
   whole sprigs
3 garlic cloves, crushed
1 tbsp coarse sea salt
1 tsp black pepper
200ml whipping cream
⅓ quantity of Crumble ↗ page 279
100g Parmesan cheese,
   freshly grated
300g cherry tomatoes,
   on the vine
1 tsp chopped flat-leaf parsley

Romano (or romero) peppers are vibrant red and have an appealing long, pointy shape. To maintain their shape and visual impact, we roast them briefly and don't peel them. This means you get a bit of skin and seeds on the plate. If you mind this, roast the peppers for another 10 minutes, place in a sealed container to cool down, and then peel and remove the seeds. The peppers will disintegrate slightly.

It is vital that you use good-quality buffalo mozzarella for this recipe. Ordinary mozzarella will just get lost with all the intense flavours. Instead of mozzarella you could use feta or small pieces of broken Parmesan. The peppers can be marinated well ahead of time and assembled just before serving.

Marinated romano peppers with buffalo mozzarella

serves 6 as a starter

1 Preheat the oven to 200°C/Gas Mark 6. Spread the peppers out on a roasting tray, drizzle with 2 tablespoons of the olive oil and sprinkle with salt and pepper. Mix well and roast for 12–15 minutes, until the peppers become tender and their skin begins to colour.
2 Meanwhile, mix together the coriander, parsley, garlic, vinegar and 80ml of the olive oil. Season liberally and taste to make sure the flavours are robust. Put the warm peppers in a bowl, pour the marinade over them, then cover and leave at room temperature for at least 2 hours.
3 To serve, lay out the peppers and rocket on a serving plate and spoon the marinade over them. Break the mozzarella into large chunks with your hands and dot it over the peppers. Drizzle with the remaining oil and garnish with parsley.

6 romano peppers
120ml olive oil
2½ tbsp finely chopped coriander
2½ tbsp finely chopped flat-leaf parsley, plus extra to garnish
1 garlic clove, crushed
3 tbsp cider vinegar
100g rocket
200g buffalo mozzarella
coarse sea salt and black pepper

This bold treatment for mushrooms, with a sharp intensity of flavour, makes a refreshing starter. Don't necessarily restrict yourself to the types of mushrooms specified. You can mix and match to suit your taste. In any case, provide some substantial chunks of bread to soak up the juices.

Mixed mushrooms with cinnamon and lemon

serves 6–8

1 First you will need to pick through the mushrooms, paring away dirt from the feet of the mushrooms and using a stiff pastry brush to clear any dirt from the caps and gills (don't be tempted to clean them in a bucket of water, as they will absorb the water and go soggy).
2 Put a large sauté pan over a medium heat and add the olive oil to heat it slightly. Sprinkle in the thyme, garlic, parsley, cinnamon sticks, salt and pepper. Lay the button, chestnut and shiitake mushrooms on top. Do not stir. Turn the heat up high and cook for 5 minutes. Only then give the pan a good shake and add the oyster mushrooms. Give a little stir and leave to cook for another 3 minutes. Turn off the heat and add the enoki mushrooms, followed by the lemon juice. Give the pan another good shake around, taste and add more salt and pepper if necessary. Serve warm or at room temperature.

400g button mushrooms
400g chestnut mushrooms
300g shiitake mushrooms
400g oyster mushrooms
200g enoki mushrooms
160ml olive oil
30g chopped thyme
10 garlic cloves, crushed
100g flat-leaf parsley, chopped
6 cinnamon sticks
25g coarse sea salt
1 tbsp coarsely ground black pepper
60ml lemon juice

This is another of Scully's creations. The mushrooms are cooked with lots of butter and herbs and then served warm with the most soothing topping. You can prepare the mushrooms and barley ahead of time, then heat them up and add the lemon, feta and herbs at the last minute.

Try your hand at preserving lemons if you have the patience (↗ page 273). Otherwise, Belazu makes them and sells them in delis or online, at www.belazu.com.

Portobello mushrooms with pearl barley and preserved lemon

serves 6 as a starter

1 First cook the barley. Heat the sunflower oil in a heavy-based saucepan and sauté the onion and garlic until translucent. Add the stock and bring to the boil. Stir in the barley, reduce the heat, then cover and simmer for 1 hour, until all the liquid has been absorbed and the barley is tender.

2 Meanwhile, preheat the oven to 180°C/Gas Mark 4. Take a large baking tray and grease it heavily with two-thirds of the butter. Scatter the sprigs of thyme over it and place the mushrooms on top, stem-side up. Pour over the wine and stock and scatter the sliced garlic over. Dot each mushroom with a couple of knobs of the remaining butter, then season with salt and pepper. Cover the tray with foil and place in the oven for 15–20 minutes, until the mushrooms are tender. Leave them in their cooking juices until you are ready to serve.

3 When the barley is done, remove the pan from the heat and stir in the preserved lemon, feta, parsley and thyme. Taste and add salt and pepper. To serve, reheat the mushrooms in the oven for a few minutes, if necessary. Place each mushroom on a serving plate, stem-side up. Scoop the barley on top and spoon some of the mushroom cooking juices over. Garnish with the basil and drizzle over the olive oil.

100g unsalted butter
15 sprigs of thyme
6 large Portobello mushrooms
180ml dry white wine
250ml vegetable stock
2 garlic cloves, finely sliced
coarse sea salt and black pepper

Pearl barley
1 tbsp sunflower oil
1 medium onion, finely chopped
1 garlic clove, finely chopped
750ml vegetable or chicken stock
110g pearl barley
1 quarter of preserved lemon, flesh removed and skin finely chopped
50g feta cheese, crumbled
1 tbsp chopped flat-leaf parsley
2 tsp thyme leaves
2 tbsp purple basil sprouts, radish sprouts, or purple basil leaves, shredded
1 tbsp olive oil

The appeal here is the complementary flavours of earth (artichokes and potatoes) and acid (lemon and tomato), with the dominant background note of the oily black olives. It goes well with most light, simply cooked main courses – fish, meat or vegetarian – served warm or at room temperature.

Jerusalem artichokes are a bit of a con – neither artichokes nor (unlike us) from Jerusalem. Still, they have a superb deep flavour that spreads throughout a whole dish. Some varieties, the tough-skinned ones resembling ginger roots, require peeling. Others are fine unpeeled as long as you slice them thinly.

Roast potatoes and Jerusalem artichokes with lemon and sage

serves 4–6

500g Jersey Royals or other small potatoes
500g Jerusalem artichokes
4 garlic cloves, crushed
50ml olive oil
2 tbsp roughly chopped sage
1 tsp salt
½ tsp black pepper
1 lemon
250g cherry tomatoes
170g Kalamata olives, pitted
2 tbsp roughly chopped flat-leaf parsley

1 Preheat the oven to 200°C/Gas Mark 6. Wash the potatoes well, put them in a large saucepan and cover with plenty of salted water. Bring to the boil and simmer for 20 minutes, until semi-cooked. Drain, cool slightly and then cut each potato in half lengthways. Put them in a large roasting tray.

2 Wash the Jerusalem artichokes, cut them into slices 5mm thick and add to the potatoes. Add the garlic, olive oil, sage, salt and pepper. Mix everything well with your hands and put in the oven.

3 Meanwhile, thinly slice the lemon and remove the pips. After the vegetables have been roasting for about 30 minutes, add the sliced lemon, stir with a wooden spoon and return to the oven for 20 minutes. Now add the cherry tomatoes and olives, stir well again and cook for a further 15 minutes.

4 Remove from the oven and stir in some of the chopped parsley. Transfer to a serving dish and garnish with the remaining parsley.

ılar in Victorian Britain, has recently made a
widely available from the early autumn throughout
nix it with the red variety to create a multicoloured
both, use only one type.
ıll with most soft herbs and is complemented by
es such as ricotta or soft goat's cheeses. Its mild
benefits from acidity, so try mixing it with fruit such
fruits.
ep well in the fridge for two days.

and golden beetroot

ven to 200°C/Gas Mark 6. Wash the beetroot well
m in foil individually. Bake in the oven for anything from
utes, depending on their size (baby beetroot might take
Check each one, as cooking times can vary a lot: the
ıould be tender when pierced with a sharp knife.
the sunflower seeds out in an ovenproof dish and toast in the
n alongside the beetroot for 8 minutes, just until lightly coloured.
3 Once the beetroot are ready, unwrap them and peel with a small knife
   while still warm. Cut each into halves, quarters or 2–3cm dice. Mix
   the beetroot with the rest of the ingredients in a bowl. Toss well and
   then taste: there should be a clear sweetness balanced by enough
   salt. Adjust the seasoning if necessary, plate, sprinkle with more
   chervil and serve.

serves 4

500g golden beetroot
500g red beetroot
80g sunflower seeds
90ml maple syrup
4 tbsp sherry vinegar
4 tbsp olive oil
2 garlic cloves, crushed
20g chervil leaves, plus more
  to garnish
60g baby chard leaves, baby
  spinach or rocket
coarse sea salt and black pepper

Somewhere between a mash and a potato-mayonnaise salad, this
dish is very satisfying both warm and at room temperature. Adjust the
seasoning and the amount of horseradish to suit your taste (re-check
once it has cooled down).

Sorrel is not always available. If necessary, substitute with rocket, or
any soft herb, and a little lemon juice. Horseradish sauce or wasabi paste
(beware, it's strong) make good alternatives to fresh horseradish. Again,
taste and judge how much you need.

Crushed new potatoes with horseradish and sorrel

1 Wash the potatoes well but don't peel them. Put them in a pan with
   plenty of salted water, bring to the boil and simmer for 25–30 minutes,
   until tender. Drain well, transfer to a large mixing bowl and, while
   they are still hot, crush them well with a fork or a potato masher. Make
   sure most of the hard lumps are crushed.
2 In another bowl, mix together the yoghurt, olive oil, garlic, horseradish
   and salt and pepper to taste. Pour this dressing over the hot potatoes,
   add the sorrel and mix well. Taste and adjust the seasoning.
3 Just before serving, garnish with the cress, spring onions and a drizzle
   of olive oil.

serves 6

1kg new potatoes
300g Greek yoghurt
100ml olive oil, plus some
  for drizzling
2 garlic cloves, crushed
25g fresh horseradish root,
  grated
4 tbsp roughly chopped
  sorrel leaves
25g garden cress (or another
  small sprouting leaf)
2 spring onions, sliced
coarse sea salt and black pepper

This winter dish demonstrates how seasonal roots can be used playfully to create the opposite of the usual weighty casseroles. It is a bit like a rémoulade in its tang, but also has multilayered sweet (dried cherries) and savoury (capers) flavours to create a magnificently intense accompaniment to fish or lamb. It also makes a great addition to a vegetarian mezze selection. A small amount will go a long way.

Variations on this dish are endless. Try using kohlrabi, beetroot, turnip, carrot or cabbage, or a combination of them. Most soft herbs would suit, and don't forget acidity from citrus juice or vinegar to lighten it up.

This particular salad will look more professional if you have a mandolin or a shredding attachment for shredding the celeriac and swede. Coarsely grating them is also perfectly fine. The flavours will not be affected.

Sweet and sour celeriac and swede

serves 4–6

1 Place the shredded celeriac and swede in a mixing bowl. Add all the rest of the ingredients and use your hands to mix everything together thoroughly. 'Massaging' the vegetables a little will help them absorb the flavours. Taste and add salt and pepper to your liking. You might also want to add some extra sugar and vinegar.

2 Allow the salad to sit for an hour so the flavours can evolve. It will keep for up to 2 days in the fridge. Add more herbs just before serving, for a fresher look.

250g celeriac, peeled and thinly shredded
250g swede, peeled and thinly shredded
4 tbsp roughly chopped flat-leaf parsley
4 tbsp roughly chopped dill
50g capers, drained and roughly chopped
4 tbsp lemon juice (about 1 large lemon)
1 tsp cider vinegar
4 tbsp olive oil
4 tbsp sunflower oil
3 tsp Dijon mustard
2 garlic cloves, crushed
2 tsp caster sugar
100g dried sour cherries
salt and black pepper

The slightly burnt onion and sweet, creamy mash create an appealing mixture of textures and soothing flavours. You could substitute turnip, celeriac, potato, carrot or sweet potato for the parsnip or pumpkin. Just keep the colours in mind.

Parsnip and pumpkin mash

serves 4–6

1 Preheat the oven to 200°C/Gas Mark 6. Toss the pumpkin or squash with the olive oil and a little salt and pepper and spread out in a roasting tray. Roast for 30–45 minutes, until soft and mashable. Once out of the oven, keep somewhere warm. Meanwhile, using a good serrated knife, cut about 1cm off the top of the garlic head and place the bottom part in the oven next to the roasting pumpkin. Bake it for approximately 30 minutes, until the cloves are completely tender.

2 While the pumpkin is roasting, cook the parsnips in boiling salted water for 30 minutes, until they are completely soft. Drain and keep warm. Pour the sunflower oil into a medium saucepan, heat well and fry the onion rings in it in 2–3 batches. They should turn brown, almost burnt. Transfer to a colander and sprinkle with salt.

3 Take a large bowl that can accommodate the whole mixture. Hold the bottom of the head of garlic and gently press upwards to release the cooked flesh into the bowl. Add the butter, nutmeg, some seasoning and then the parsnips. Crush well, using a potato masher. Add the cooked pumpkin and mash very lightly (use a fork). Don't over-mix; the mash should remain chunky and the pumpkin and parsnip distinct.

4 Gently fold in the crème fraîche and chives to form a ripple in the mash. Spoon a mound on to each serving plate, garnish with the fried onions and a drizzle of olive oil and serve at once.

600g (peeled weight) pumpkin or butternut squash, cut into 2–3cm dice
3 tbsp olive oil, plus extra for drizzling
1 head of garlic
5 medium parsnips, peeled and cut into large chunks
200ml sunflower oil
2 onions, sliced into rings
80g unsalted butter
1 tsp ground nutmeg
300g crème fraîche, at room temperature
15g chives, roughly chopped
salt and black pepper

This recipe is the exact opposite of what's typically associated with its name: crunchy carrots, fresh peas and lots of robust flavours of sweet and spice. Excellent served hot for Christmas dinner (omitting the pea shoots), or as a light spring salad.

Carrot and peas

serves 6

1 Start by making the sweet sauce for roasting the carrots. Pour the orange juice, wine and honey into a saucepan, add the cinnamon and star anise and bring to a simmer. Cook gently, uncovered, for 20–40 minutes (depending on the size of your pan and the heat level), until reduced to about a third. Set aside.

2 Preheat the oven to 230°C/Gas Mark 8. Heat a small frying pan, add the coriander seeds and dry toast them over a high heat for about 3 minutes. Put the seeds in a bowl and mix with the carrots, olive oil, garlic and some salt and pepper. Spread the mixture out on a large baking tray and put in the oven. After about 15 minutes (the carrots should have taken on some serious colour by now), remove the tray carefully, add the sweet sauce (including the cinnamon and star anise), stir well and return to the oven for about 7 minutes, until the carrots are cooked through but still have a bit of bite. Remove from the oven and allow them to cool down.

3 Throw the peas into a pot containing plenty of boiling salted water and simmer for a minute. Drain at once into a colander, run under a cold tap to stop the cooking and then leave to drain thoroughly.

4 Before serving, gently stir together the carrots and peas. Taste and add more salt and pepper if you like. Dot with the pea shoots as you pile the vegetables on to a serving plate.

130ml orange juice
60ml red wine
50g honey
2 cinnamon sticks
4 star anise
1½ tbsp coriander seeds
1kg carrots, peeled and cut at an angle into slices 1cm thick
90ml olive oil
3 garlic cloves, crushed
450g shelled peas, fresh or frozen
75g pea shoots (use lamb's lettuce, if unavailable)
salt and pepper

You might think this recipe doesn't sound right. It didn't sound quite right to us either when we came across it on the highly useful recipe site, www.epicurious.com. The idea of adding maple syrup and sultanas to an (already) sweet potato and then mixing lots of herbs and spices in as well just couldn't be right … unless you are an American. But we were somehow tempted to try it and it did work, creating a vivid and intense mix of tastes and textures.

This version boasts additional old favourites of ours: chilli and coriander. Try it as a side dish at your Christmas table or as an original picnic salad.

Roasted sweet potato with pecan and maple

serves 4

1 Preheat the oven to 190°C/Gas Mark 5. Start with the sweet potatoes. Don't peel them! Cut them into 2cm cubes, spread them out on a baking tray and drizzle with the olive oil. Sprinkle with some salt and pepper, mix well with your hands and then roast in the oven for about 30 minutes, until just tender. Turn them over gently half way through cooking.
2 In a separate baking tray, toast the pecans for 5 minutes. Remove from the oven and chop roughly.
3 To make the dressing, whisk together all the ingredients in a small bowl with some salt and pepper. Taste and adjust the seasoning, if necessary.
4 When the potatoes are ready, transfer them to a large bowl while still hot. Add the spring onions, parsley, coriander, chilli, pecans and sultanas. Pour the dressing over and toss gently to blend, then season to taste. Serve at once or at room temperature.

2 sweet potatoes
   (about 850g in total)
3 tbsp olive oil
35g pecan nuts
4 spring onions, roughly
   chopped
4 tbsp roughly chopped flat-leaf
   parsley
2 tbsp roughly chopped coriander
¼ tsp dried chilli flakes
35g sultanas
salt and pepper

Dressing
4 tbsp olive oil
2 tbsp maple syrup
1 tbsp sherry vinegar
1 tbsp lemon juice
2 tbsp orange juice
2 tsp grated fresh ginger
½ tsp ground cinnamon

This comforting dish was created by Danielle Postma, who is now back home in South Africa running her own blossoming food business, Moema's. We would have loved to take some credit for Danielle's success but she actually had it all before coming to Ottolenghi. Danielle's big personality and warmth make everybody fall in love with her in an instant. She has a natural gift for presentation and, like herself, her food constantly smiles.

This dish is simple but effective, due to the way the potatoes are arranged in the baking dish. You can prepare everything a day in advance and have it ready in the fridge to just pop in the oven. The sage can be replaced with thyme, or you could use both. Make sure you choose orange-fleshed sweet potatoes (as opposed to the paler variety).

Danielle's sweet potato gratin

serves 4–6

1 Preheat the oven to 200°C/Gas Mark 6. Wash the sweet potatoes (do not peel them) and cut them into discs 5mm thick. A mandolin is best for this job but you could use a sharp knife.

2 In a bowl, mix together the sweet potatoes, sage, garlic, salt and pepper. Arrange the slices of sweet potato in a deep, medium-sized ovenproof dish by taking tight packs of them and standing them up next to each other. They should fit together quite tightly so you get parallel lines of sweet potato slices (skins showing) along the length or width of the dish. Throw any remaining bits of garlic or sage from the bowl over the potatoes. Cover the dish with foil, place in the oven and roast for 45 minutes. Remove the foil and pour the cream evenly over the potatoes. Roast, uncovered, for a further 25 minutes. The cream should have thickened by now. Stick a sharp knife in different places in the dish to make sure the potatoes are cooked. They should be totally soft.

3 Serve immediately, garnished with sage, or leave to cool down. In any case, bringing the potatoes to the table in the baking dish, after scraping the outside clean, will make a strong impact.

6 medium sweet potatoes (about 1.5kg in total)
5 tbsp roughly chopped sage, plus extra to garnish
6 garlic cloves, crushed
2 tsp coarse sea salt
½ tsp freshly ground black pepper
250ml whipping cream

Butterbeans with sweet chilli sauce and fresh herbs

serves 6

A colourful salad, both in appearance and flavour. It is well worth planning ahead and soaking the butterbeans overnight. Freshly cooked, they have a silky, rich texture, just as the name implies. Serve at a weekend brunch, with grilled lamb for example.

400g dried butterbeans
6 garlic cloves, crushed
70ml sweet chilli sauce
2 tbsp sesame oil
3 tbsp soy sauce
3 tbsp lemon juice
2 red peppers, halved, deseeded and cut into 2cm squares
4 spring onions, white and green bits, chopped
35g coriander, chopped
30g mint leaves, chopped
coarse sea salt and black pepper

1   Put the butterbeans in a large bowl and fill with enough water to cover them by twice their volume. Leave to soak overnight at room temperature.

2   The next day, drain the beans and place in a large saucepan. Cover with plenty of cold water and bring to a simmer. Cook for 35–55 minutes, skimming froth from the surface and topping up with boiling water if necessary, until tender. The cooking time will vary according to the bean size and freshness, so try them a few times during cooking to make sure they don't turn to a mush. In case they begin to overcook, remove from the heat and add plenty of cold water to the pan to stop the cooking. When they are done, drain in a colander and leave to one side.

3   While the beans are cooking, make the sauce. Place the crushed garlic in a bowl large enough to hold the beans. Add the sweet chilli sauce, sesame oil, soy sauce and lemon juice and mix well with a small whisk. Add the red peppers, season the mixture with salt and pepper and set aside.

4   Once the beans have cooled down slightly but are still warm, add them to the sauce, together with the spring onions, herbs and plenty of seasoning. Mix gently with your hands. Taste and adjust the seasoning. Eat warm or cold – just remember to readjust the seasoning before serving.

Don't be put off by the healthfood-shop connotations whole wheat may have. This is a highly refreshing salad. Its biting astringency and light sweetness make it a perfect companion to plainly barbecued meat or fish. On its own, it makes a modest vegetarian main course.

Whole wheat needs soaking for a good 14–18 hours. If you didn't plan ahead, substitute it with pearl barley, following the cooking instructions on the packet. Thanks to Helen for the inspiration.

Whole wheat and mushrooms with celery and shallots

serves 4

200g whole wheat grains
3 tbsp soft brown sugar
50ml good-quality sherry vinegar
2–3 shallots, finely chopped
3 celery stalks, finely chopped
200g button mushrooms,
  sliced 5mm thick
40g flat-leaf parsley leaves
10g tarragon leaves
50ml olive oil
coarse sea salt and black pepper

1 Wash the wheat in plenty of cold water, then transfer to a large bowl and cover with fresh water. Leave to soak overnight.

2 The next day, drain the wheat, put it in a large pan with plenty of fresh water to cover and simmer for 45–60 minutes. The grains should have now softened up but still have a bite. Drain in a colander and leave to cool.

3 You need to make the dressing at least an hour before serving the salad. Whisk together the sugar and vinegar until the sugar has completely dissolved. Add the shallots and celery and leave to marinate.

4 To assemble the salad, put the mushrooms in a mixing bowl and toss with the dressing. Add the wheat and then tear in the parsley leaves. Add the whole tarragon leaves, plus the olive oil and some salt and pepper. Taste, adjust the seasoning accordingly and serve.

Camargue red rice and quinoa with orange and pistachios (↗ page 76)

Couscous and mograbiah with oven-dried tomatoes (↗ page 77)

Tricia Jadoonanan, for a long period the head chef at our Islington branch, brought Camargue red rice to Ottolenghi and does wonders with it, including this recipe. This French rice has an outstanding nutty flavour, a good dry consistency and a colour much more appealing than other wholegrain varieties.

Quinoa, a native of South America, has a satisfying 'bouncy' texture and is probably one of the healthiest foodstuffs available. It has more protein than any other grain and the perfect set of amino acids (not that this would make us eat it if it didn't taste great).

Camargue red rice and quinoa with orange and pistachios

serves 4

1 Preheat the oven to 170°C/Gas Mark 3. Spread the pistachios out on a baking tray and toast for 8 minutes, until lightly coloured. Remove from the oven, allow to cool slightly and then chop roughly. Set aside.

2 Fill 2 saucepans with salted water and bring to the boil. Simmer the quinoa in one for 12–14 minutes and the rice in the other for 20 minutes. Both should be tender but still have a bite. Drain in a sieve and spread out the 2 grains separately on flat trays to hasten the cooling down.

3 While the grains are cooking, sauté the white onion in 4 tablespoons of the olive oil for 10–12 minutes, stirring occasionally, until golden brown. Leave to cool completely.

4 In a large mixing bowl combine the rice, quinoa, cooked onion and the remaining oil. Add all the rest of the ingredients, then taste and adjust the seasoning. Serve at room temperature.

60g shelled pistachio nuts
200g quinoa
200g Camargue red rice
1 medium onion, sliced
150ml olive oil
grated zest and juice of 1 orange
2 tsp lemon juice
1 garlic clove, crushed
4 spring onions, thinly sliced
100g dried apricots, roughly
**   chopped**
40g rocket
salt and black pepper

Mograbiah is a large variety of couscous, made from durum wheat semolina and is common throughout the Arab world. It is also known as pearl or giant couscous and, in North Africa, as berkukis. Unlike ordinary couscous, it can be found only in specialist Arab shops in the UK. We buy it from Green Valley, the luscious Middle Eastern supermarket just off London's Edgware Road. If you can't get hold of it, try to find the Sardinian equivalent, fregola, which is stocked by some Italian delis. If all this leads you nowhere, use couscous only (making the quantity below up to 500g). You will lose out a little on the interesting combination of textures but still enjoy the explosive mix of flavours.

The dried tomatoes are a great store cupboard ingredient. Keep them immersed in oil if you want them to last a long time. The caramelised onion is also handy to have in the fridge. It will keep there for at least five days and makes a great addition to omelettes, quiches, bruschetta, pasta – anything, really.

Couscous and mograbiah with oven-dried tomatoes

serves 6–8

16 large, ripe plum tomatoes,
  cut into halves lengthways
2 tbsp muscovado sugar
150ml olive oil
2 tbsp balsamic vinegar
2 onions, thinly sliced
250g mograbiah
400ml chicken or vegetable stock
a pinch of saffron strands
250g couscous
1 tbsp picked tarragon leaves
1 tbsp nigella seeds
100g Labneh ↗ page 272
coarse sea salt and black pepper

1   Preheat the oven to 150°C/Gas Mark 2. Arrange the tomato halves on a baking tray, skin-side down, and sprinkle with the sugar, 2 tablespoons of the olive oil, plus the balsamic vinegar and some salt and pepper. Place in the oven and bake for 2 hours or until the tomatoes have lost most of their moisture.

2   Meanwhile, put the onions in a large pan with 4 tablespoons of the olive oil and sauté over a high heat for 10–12 minutes, stirring occasionally, until they are a dark golden colour.

3   Throw the mograbiah into a large pan of boiling salted water (as for cooking pasta). Simmer for 15 minutes, until it is soft but still retains a bite; some varieties might take less time, so check the instructions on the packet. Drain well and rinse under cold water.

4   In a separate pot, bring the stock to the boil with the saffron and a little salt. Place the couscous in a large bowl and add 3 tablespoons of the olive oil and the boiling stock. Cover with cling film and leave for 10 minutes.

5   Once ready, mix the couscous with a fork or a whisk to get rid of any lumps and to fluff it up. Add the cooked mograbiah, the tomatoes and their juices, the onions and their oil, plus the tarragon and half the nigella seeds. Taste and adjust the seasoning and oil. It is likely that it will need a fair amount of salt. Allow the dish to come to room temperature. To serve, arrange it gently on a serving plate, place the labneh on top (in balls or spoonfuls), drizzle with the remaining oil and finish with the rest of the nigella seeds.

Adding lots of 'wet' elements, as we do here, prevents cold couscous from turning into a dry mouthful. You can keep on piling in the herbs (chervil, coriander, chives – they all work), the more the merrier.

Couscous with dried apricots and butternut squash

serves 4

1 Preheat the oven to 180°C/Gas Mark 4. Place the onion in a large frying pan with 2 tablespoons of the oil and a pinch of salt. Sauté over a high heat, stirring frequently, for about 10 minutes, until golden brown. Set aside.
2 Meanwhile, pour enough hot water from the tap over the apricots just to cover them. Soak for 5 minutes, then drain and cut into 5mm dice.
3 Mix the diced squash with 1 tablespoon of the olive oil and some salt and pepper. Spread the squash out on a baking tray, place in the oven and bake for about 25 minutes, until lightly coloured and quite soft.
4 While waiting for the butternut squash, cook the couscous. Bring the stock to the boil with the saffron. Place the couscous in a large heatproof bowl and pour the boiling stock over it, plus the remaining olive oil. Cover with cling film and leave for about 10 minutes; all the liquid should have been absorbed.
5 Use a fork or a whisk to fluff up the couscous, then add the onion, butternut squash, apricots, herbs, cinnamon and lemon zest. Mix well with your hands, trying not mash the butternut squash. Taste and add salt and pepper if necessary. Serve warmish or cold.

1 large onion, thinly sliced
6 tbsp olive oil
50g dried apricots
1 small butternut squash
  (about 450g), peeled, seeded
  and cut into 2cm dice
250g couscous
400ml chicken or vegetable stock
a pinch of saffron strands
3 tbsp roughly chopped tarragon
3 tbsp roughly chopped mint
3 tbsp roughly chopped
  flat-leaf parsley
1½ tsp ground cinnamon
grated zest of ½ lemon
coarse sea salt and black pepper

Sweet, sour and musky-salty, there are many contrasting flavours in this dish, yet it still ends up harmoniously synchronised – the sweet and acid hitting first, followed by a mellowing savoury taste. It makes a heady starter.

Puy lentils with sour cherries, bacon and Gorgonzola

serves 2–4 as a starter

1 Wash the lentils under cold running water and then drain. Transfer to a saucepan and add enough water to cover them by 3 times their height. Add the bay leaves, bring to the boil and then simmer for about 20 minutes, until the lentils are al dente.

2 Meanwhile, make the sauce. Place the shallots in a pan with 2 tablespoons of the olive oil and sauté over a medium heat for about 10 minutes, until golden. Add the water, sugar, cherries and vinegar and continue simmering over a low heat for 8–10 minutes, until you get a thick sauce. Taste and season with salt and pepper.

3 Drain the lentils well and immediately add them to the sauce so they can soak up all the flavours. Stir together, taste and adjust the salt again. It will need quite a lot, but remember you are adding bacon and Gorgonzola later, which are salty. Set aside to cool down.

4 Heat the remaining olive oil in a saucepan and fry the bacon in it for 3 minutes on each side, until it turns quite crisp. Transfer to a piece of kitchen paper to cool. Tear the bacon into large pieces and add to the lentils, then add the spinach and stir well. Taste and see if the salad needs any more oil, salt or pepper.

5 Transfer to serving plates and dot with broken chunks of Gorgonzola.

125g Puy lentils
2 bay leaves
2–3 shallots, finely chopped
3 tbsp olive oil
3 tbsp water
1 tsp caster sugar
60g dried sour cherries
70ml red wine vinegar
8 streaky bacon rashers
80g baby spinach
120g creamy Gorgonzola cheese
salt and black pepper

Don't be put off by what may seem like a carbohydrate overkill. The soft, warm sweet potato almost melts over the chickpeas, while the yoghurt sauce lightens them with its velvety smoothness. The result is an extremely satisfying vegetarian main course.

In her book, *Amaretto, Apple Cake and Artichokes* (Vintage, 2006), Anna Del Conte suggests adding a paste of bicarbonate of soda, flour and salt to chickpeas when soaking them, in order to soften very hard skins. (We can't recommend this book enough for the most thorough introduction to Italian ingredients and methods.) In most cases bicarbonate of soda alone does the trick. No matter what you do, you will need to soak chickpeas for at least 12 hours and up to 24 before cooking them.

Chickpeas and spinach with honeyed sweet potato

serves 6–8

1 Start the night before by putting the chickpeas in a large bowl. Fill with enough cold water to cover the chickpeas by twice their height. Add the bicarbonate of soda and leave to soak overnight at room temperature.
2 The next day, drain and rinse the chickpeas, place them in a large saucepan and cover with plenty of fresh water. Bring to the boil, then reduce the heat and simmer for 1–1½ hours (they could take much longer in extreme cases). They should be totally tender but retain their shape. Occasionally you will need to skim the froth off the surface. You might also need to top up the pan with boiling water so the chickpeas remain submerged. When they are ready, drain them in a colander and set aside.
3 Put the sweet potatoes in a wide saucepan with the water, butter, honey and salt. Bring to the boil, then reduce the heat and simmer for 35–40 minutes, until the potatoes are tender and most of the liquid has been absorbed. Turn them over half way through the cooking to colour evenly. Remove from the heat and keep warm.
4 While the sweet potatoes are cooking, prepare the sauce for the chickpeas. Heat the olive oil in a large frying pan and add the onion, cumin seeds and coriander seeds. Fry for 8 minutes, while stirring, until golden brown. Add the tomato purée, cook for a minute while you stir and then add the tomatoes, sugar and ground cumin. Continue cooking for about 5 minutes over a medium heat. Taste and season with salt and pepper.
5 Stir the spinach into the tomato sauce, then add the cooked chickpeas. Mix together and cook for another 5 minutes. Taste again and adjust the seasoning.
6 Make the yoghurt sauce by whisking together all the ingredients. Season with salt and pepper to taste.
7 To serve, spoon the warm chickpeas into a serving dish, arrange the sweet potato slices on top and garnish with the coriander leaves. Spoon the yoghurt sauce on top or serve on the side.

200g dried chickpeas
1 tsp bicarbonate of soda
2 tbsp olive oil
1 onion, finely chopped
1 tsp cumin seeds
1 tsp coriander seeds
1 tbsp tomato purée
400g Italian tinned tomatoes, chopped
1 tsp caster sugar
1½ tsp ground cumin
100g baby spinach leaves
10g coriander leaves, to garnish
salt and black pepper

Honeyed sweet potato
500g sweet potatoes, peeled and cut into slices 2.5cm thick
700ml water
50g unsalted butter
4 tbsp honey
½ tsp salt

Yoghurt sauce
100g Greek yoghurt
1 garlic clove, crushed
juice and grated zest of 1 lemon
3 tbsp olive oil
1 tsp dried mint

This lentil and rice dish is one of the most popular in Egypt, sold hot by street vendors and specialist restaurants. It is not too far removed from the Indian *kitchari,* ancestor to the British kedgeree. Usually in Egypt it is served with a spicy tomato sauce, but it's also delicious with cucumber, tomato and yoghurt salad.

Kosheri

serves 4

1 Start with the sauce. Heat the olive oil in a saucepan, add the garlic and chillies and fry for 2 minutes. Add the chopped tomatoes, water, vinegar, salt and cumin. Bring to the boil, then reduce the heat and simmer for 20 minutes, until slightly thickened. Remove the sauce from the heat, stir in the coriander and then taste. See if you want to add any salt, pepper or extra coriander. Keep hot or leave to cool; both ways will work with the hot kosheri. Just remember to adjust the seasoning again when cold.

2 To make the kosheri, place the lentils in a large sieve and wash them under a cold running tap. Transfer to a large saucepan, cover with plenty of cold water and bring to the boil. Reduce the heat and simmer for 25 minutes. The lentils should be tender but far from mushy. Drain in a colander and leave to one side.

3 In a large bowl, cover the rice with cold water, wash and then drain well. Melt the butter in a large saucepan over a medium heat. Add the raw vermicelli, stir, and continue frying and stirring until the vermicelli turns golden brown. Add the drained rice and mix well until it is coated in the butter. Now add the stock or water, nutmeg, cinnamon, salt and pepper. Bring to the boil, cover and then reduce the heat to a minimum and simmer for 12 minutes. Turn off the heat, remove the lid, cover the pan with a clean tea towel and put the lid back on. Leave like that for about 5 minutes; this helps make the rice light and fluffy.

4 Heat the olive oil in a large frying pan, add the onions and sauté over a medium heat for about 20 minutes, until dark brown. Transfer to kitchen paper to drain.

5 To serve, lightly break up the rice with a fork and then add the lentils and most of the onions, reserving a few for garnish. Taste for seasoning and adjust accordingly. Pile the rice high on a serving platter and top with the remaining onions. Serve hot, with the tomato sauce.

300g green lentils
200g basmati rice
40g unsalted butter
50g vermicelli noodles,
**   broken into 4cm pieces**
400ml chicken stock or water
½ tsp grated nutmeg
1½ tsp ground cinnamon
1½ tsp salt
½ tsp black pepper
4 tbsp olive oil
2 white onions, halved and
**   thinly sliced**

Spicy tomato sauce
4 tbsp olive oil
2 garlic cloves, crushed
2 hot red chillies, seeded and
**   finely diced**
8 ripe tomatoes, chopped
**   (tinned are fine)**
370ml water
4 tbsp cider vinegar
3 tsp salt
2 tsp ground cumin
20g coriander leaves, chopped

Stuffing vegetables is a rare culinary experience in these busy days. It is time consuming and gives a pleasure that we don't often experience any more – the kind of bliss that results from communal cooking, when time is not an object and the purpose is the process as well as the end result.

Luckily, we were fortunate enough to experience this when Tamara Meitlis, mother of our designer/partner Alex, visited us recently and taught us some old secrets of Turkish cookery … and patience. This is one of them.

These vine leaves are so moreish you might want to double the recipe.

Tamara's stuffed vine leaves

1 First prepare the filling. Heat the olive oil in a medium saucepan, add the onion and sauté over a medium heat for 8 minutes or until softened but not coloured. Add the rice and cook for 2 minutes, stirring to coat it in the oil. Add all the remaining filling ingredients and cook over a medium heat for 10 minutes, stirring from time to time (the mixture should be sweet and sour, the rice still hard). Remove from the heat and leave to cool.

2 Pour boiling water over the vine leaves and leave to soak for 10 minutes. Remove the vine leaves from the water and pat dry. Using a pair of kitchen scissors, cut the stalks from the leaves. Put any torn or unusable leaves in the bottom of a medium heavy-based saucepan, making sure it is covered with a layer of leaves a few millimetres thick. This will prevent the stuffed leaves from burning later.

3 To fill and roll the vine leaves, choose medium leaves, roughly 13cm wide (you can cut them to this size with scissors, if necessary). If possible, use fine, pale leaves, not dark, thick ones. Place a leaf on a work surface, the beautiful veiny side down, and spoon about ¾ teaspoon of the filling in the centre-bottom of the leaf, steering clear of the edges. Take the 2 sides and fold them tightly over the rice. Now roll neatly towards the top of the leaf, ending with a tight, short cigar. They should be small – roughly 3 x 1cm.

4 Repeat with all the leaves and arrange inside the lined saucepan in neat layers. They should fit quite tightly. Pour in enough water just to cover, then add the olive oil, lemon juice and salt. Place a small plate or saucer on top to prevent the leaves moving during cooking. Bring to a gentle boil, cover and cook on the lowest possible heat for 50–60 minutes, until the leaves are tender and almost no cooking liquid is left. You may need to add a little more boiling water during cooking.

5 Transfer the stuffed vine leaves to a serving platter and set aside to cool down. Serve cold, with the yoghurt if you like.

makes about 20 small rolls

20–25 pickled vine leaves, plus extra for lining the pan
½ tbsp olive oil
1 tbsp lemon juice
¼ tsp salt
150g full-fat yoghurt or goat's milk yoghurt (optional)

Filling
1 tbsp olive oil
1 onion, finely chopped
110g short grain rice (pudding rice is best)
1½ tbsp lemon juice
2½ tbsp currants
2 tbsp pine nuts
2 tbsp chopped flat-leaf parsley
½ tsp ground allspice (pimento)
¼ tsp ground cinnamon
¼ tsp ground cloves
½ tsp dried mint
½ tsp salt
a generous grinding of black pepper

We love chard and hope more people in the UK will learn to enjoy its earthy, lemony flavour, which surpasses that of spinach. Here it is mixed with lentils and spices to create a highly aromatic soup that will instantly win you many admirers. The lemon at the end is essential.

Red lentil and chard soup

serves 6

1 Wash the lentils in plenty of cold water. Place in a large saucepan with 2.5 litres of water, bring to the boil and simmer for 35 minutes or until soft. Skim off any scum that rises to the surface during cooking.

2 Using a slotted spoon, remove about half the lentils from the cooking liquid and set aside in a bowl. Add a generous pinch of salt to the lentils and water in the pan and liquidise using a stick blender or in a food processor. Return the reserved lentils to the soup.

3 Now comes the arduous chopping part of the recipe. Peel the red onions, halve and thinly slice them. Place a frying pan over a medium heat, add the olive oil and onions and cook, stirring occasionally, for 4–5 minutes, until the onions soften and become translucent. Meanwhile, remove and discard the large stems from the Swiss chard. Wash and rinse the leaves thoroughly, then chop them roughly. Do the same with the coriander, leaving a few whole leaves for garnish later, and that's all the chopping done.

4 Mix the cooked onions, chard leaves and chopped coriander into the lentil soup and season with the cumin, cinnamon and some salt and pepper to taste. Reheat the soup and simmer gently for 5 minutes.

5 In a pestle and mortar, or using the heel of a large knife, crush the coriander seeds and garlic together. Melt the butter gently in a small saucepan over a medium heat, add the garlic and coriander seeds and fry for 2 minutes, until the garlic starts to colour slightly. Stir this into the soup, remove the pot from the stove and cover with a lid. Leave the soup to infuse for 5 minutes before serving.

6 Serve garnished with lemon zest and coriander leaves and pass round some sourdough bread and lemon wedges. Make sure everybody squeezes the lemon into their soup.

500g split red lentils
2.5 litres cold water
2 medium red onions
2 tbsp olive oil
200g Swiss chard
50g coriander leaves
2 tsp ground cumin
1 tsp ground cinnamon
1 tbsp coriander seeds
3 garlic cloves, crushed
50g unsalted butter
grated zest of ½ lemon
sourdough bread
4 lemons, cut into wedges
salt and black pepper

Creamy, lemony and comforting, here is something you can easily get hooked on. The recipe is based, again, on burning an aubergine to get a deep, smoky flavour (↗ Burnt aubergine with yellow pepper and red onion, page 27), which enhances and yet balances the sharper notes.

Grilled aubergine and lemon soup

serves 4–6

1 First you need to grill 2 of the aubergines to impart the smoky flavour necessary for this soup. If you have a gas hob, cover your stovetop with foil and place the whole aubergines directly on 2 separate open flames. Using a pair of metal tongs, turn the aubergines regularly until the skin becomes crisp and the aubergines are very soft – about 15 minutes. Remove to a bowl and leave to cool. (If you don't have a gas hob, place the aubergines under a hot grill for roughly an hour, turning them occasionally. Don't worry if they burst slightly during the cooking.)

2 Cut the remaining aubergine into 2cm cubes. Put a large frying pan over a moderate heat and pour in half the oil. When it is hot, add half the aubergine cubes and fry, turning with a wooden spoon, until brown on all sides. Drain on kitchen paper and sprinkle with a little salt. Repeat the process with the rest of the aubergine cubes and the remaining oil.

3 When the grilled aubergines have cooled down a little, make an incision along each one and spoon out the cooked flesh, avoiding any black bits of skin. Chop the flesh roughly with a large knife and place in a saucepan with the stock, lemon juice and roughly 1½ teaspoons of salt and 1 teaspoon of pepper. Bring to the boil, then reduce the heat and simmer for 30 minutes. Add the fried aubergine cubes and cook for a further 5 minutes. Taste the soup and adjust the seasoning if needed.

4 To serve, mix the cream into the hot soup and ladle into warm bowls. Tear the basil leaves and scatter them on top.

3 large aubergines (about 1.4kg in total)
120ml sunflower oil
1 litre chicken or vegetable stock
2 tbsp lemon juice
70ml double cream
10 basil leaves
salt and black pepper

Clockwise from top left corner: Grilled aubergine and lemon soup, Chilled red pepper soup, Jerusalem artichoke and rocket soup, Harira, Red lentil and chard soup

The yoghurt gives this soup a light freshness. Adding it to the cooked soup requires tempering (which sounds much more complicated than it actually is) to prevent it splitting. Make sure that once the yoghurt is added, you don't bring the soup to a rapid boil.

Jerusalem artichoke and rocket soup

serves 4

1 Peel the artichokes with a potato peeler, wash them thoroughly and cut into 1cm dice, not too perfect. Put them in a large saucepan with the rocket, stock, garlic and a couple of pinches of salt. Bring to the boil and then simmer lightly for 25 minutes, until the artichokes are tender; insert a small knife in one to make sure they are totally soft.

2 While the soup is cooking, cut the spring onions in half lengthways and then cut across these lengths into small dice. Set aside. Break the egg into a large mixing bowl and whisk well with the yoghurt.

3 When you are ready to serve the soup, reheat it to boiling point. Take a ladleful of hot soup and whisk it into the yoghurt mix, stirring constantly. Repeat a few times, using about half the soup. You need to bring up the temperature of the yoghurt. Now pour the warm yoghurt into the soup pan, whisking constantly. Bring back to a very(!) gentle boil and leave there for a minute or two.

4 Taste the soup and season with plenty of salt and pepper. Stir in the spring onions and serve garnished with rocket.

400g Jerusalem artichokes
45g rocket, roughly chopped, plus extra to garnish
1 litre chicken or vegetable stock
10 garlic cloves, crushed
6 spring onions
1 free-range egg
350g Greek yoghurt
salt and pepper

Chilled red pepper soup with soured cream

serves 4

1 Peel the onion and chop it roughly. Heat up the oil in a large saucepan. Add the onion and sage and sauté on medium heat for 5 minutes or until the onion is translucent.

2 While the onion is cooking, halve the peppers lengthways. Take a half of one pepper, remove the seeds and white flesh and cut it into 1.5cm dice. Keep it for later.

3 Remove the seeds from the rest of the peppers, roughly chop them and stir into the saucepan with the onions. Add ¾ a teaspoon of salt, bay leaves, ground cumin, sugar and chilli.

4 Sauté for another 5 minutes. Add the stock and bring to a light simmer. Cover the pot and cook on a very low heat for 15 minutes.

5 Once the peppers are soft, remove the bay leaves from the soup. While still hot, use a liquidiser or a hand stick blender to pulverise the soup until it is totally smooth. This may take a few minutes. Leave to cool down a little.

6 Once the soup is just warm, stir in the celery, diced red pepper, lemon zest and garlic. Leave until it comes to room temperature and then refrigerate for a few hours or overnight.

7 Remove the soup from the fridge half an hour before serving. Stir well, taste and adjust the seasoning. Divide into serving bowls, sprinkle over a generous amount of chopped basil and parsley, add a spoonful of sour cream per portion and finish with a drizzle of olive oil.

1 large onion
3 tbsp olive oil, plus extra to finish
8 sage leaves, finely chopped
4 large red peppers
2 bay leaves
2 tsp ground cumin
1 tsp caster sugar
pinch of dried chilli flakes
500ml chicken or vegetable stock
1 celery stick, cut into 1.5cm dice
grated zest of ½ lemon
1 garlic clove, crushed
25g basil leaves, roughly chopped
10g flat-leaf parsley, roughly chopped
100g soured cream
salt

This is a variation on the traditional Moroccan harira soup, flavoured in the same way but without the extra carbs that are often added in the form of rice or pasta. Traditionally a meal for breaking the Ramadan fast, this hearty dish is perfect on a cold winter's evening. You can also use canned chickpeas here (roughly 500g), instead of dried.

We dedicate the recipe to Khalid Assyb, our pastry genius, who has been tormented by our constant eating through many Ramadans.

Harira (lamb, chickpeas and spinach)

serves 4–6

1 Start preparing the soup the night before by putting the dried chickpeas in a large bowl with the bicarbonate of soda and covering them with plenty of cold water – it should cover the chickpeas by at least twice their height. Leave at room temperature to soak overnight.
2 The next day, drain the soaked chickpeas, place in a large saucepan and cover with plenty of fresh water. Bring to the boil and simmer for about 1–1½ hours, until the chickpeas are tender. Drain through a colander and leave to one side.
3 Place a large saucepan over a medium heat and add the olive oil. Add the onion and fry until soft and translucent. Increase the heat, add the diced lamb and cook for 2–3 minutes, until the lamb is sealed on all sides and has taken on a bit of colour. Add the tomato purée and sugar and mix well. Cook for 2 minutes, then add the chopped tomatoes, drained chickpeas, stock or water and some salt and pepper.
4 Bring the soup to the boil and reduce the heat to a simmer. Use a large spoon to skim off any scum that forms on the surface, then cook for about 35 minutes, until the meat is tender.
5 Squeeze the lemon juice into the soup. Season the soup with the ground cumin, ginger and saffron. Taste and adjust the salt and pepper.
6 When ready to serve, bring the soup back to the boil. Wash and drain the spinach leaves and chop them roughly. Add the spinach and coriander to the soup just before you bring it to the table. Serve with a wedge of lemon.

200g dried chickpeas
1 tsp bicarbonate of soda
3 tbsp olive oil
1 large onion, cut into 1cm dice
200g lamb neck fillet, cut into 1cm dice
2 tbsp tomato purée
1 tbsp caster sugar
1kg tinned chopped tomatoes
1.2 litres chicken stock or water
juice of 1 lemon
1 tsp ground cumin
1 tsp ground ginger
a pinch of saffron strands
100g baby spinach
4 tbsp roughly chopped coriander
4–6 lemon wedges
salt and black pepper

Meat and fish

Chapter 2 Meat and fish

Sweet and sour, hot or cold, this lamb will satisfy everybody and is dead easy to make if you plan a day ahead. It is also multifunctional: an impressive main course; served as individual cutlets on a picnic; barbecued outdoors; a sandwich filling (try with the Italian bread ↗ page 162 and mayonnaise ↗ page 273) – anything goes.

Marinated rack of lamb with coriander and honey

serves 4

1 Make sure most of the fat is trimmed off the lamb, leaving a uniform thin layer that will keep the meat moist and add to the flavour. Use a very sharp knife to separate the rack into portions of 2 or 3 cutlets. Place in a non-metal container.
2 Blitz together all the remaining ingredients in a blender or food processor. Pour them over the lamb and make sure it is well covered for a night in the marinade. Refrigerate overnight.
3 Preheat the oven to 200°C/Gas Mark 6. Heat up a heavy cast iron pan, preferably a griddle pan. Remove the meat from the marinade and shake off the excess. Sear well on all sides, about 5 minutes in total. Transfer to a baking tray and cook in the oven for about 15 minutes, depending on the size of the racks and how well you want them cooked.
4 Meanwhile, heat the marinade in a small saucepan and simmer for 5 minutes. Put the cutlets on serving plates and serve the sauce in a separate bowl. Both cutlets and sauce can be served hot or at room temperature.

1kg rack of lamb, French trimmed (you can ask your butcher to do this)
20g flat leaf parsley, leaves and stalks
30g mint, leaves and stalks
30g coriander, leaves and stalks
4 garlic cloves, peeled
15g fresh ginger, peeled and sliced
3 chillies, seeded
½ tsp salt
50ml lemon juice
60ml soy sauce
120ml sunflower oil
3 tbsp honey
2 tbsp red wine vinegar
4 tbsp water

Every person that has ever worked with Ramael Scully, our evening chef in Islington, ended up adoring him for the rare combination of a seriously great talent – both in creation and faultless execution – and a warm, modest and peaceful presonality. Scully was born in Malaysia and grew up and trained as a chef in Australia. His multi-faceted ethnic background (Malay, Chinese, Indian and even Scottish) comes out as a clear solid voice through his magical cooking. Here is another one of Scully's brilliant flavour combinations, and a good option for a main course for a fancy dinner party. Everything, apart from the meat, can be prepared in advance ready to serve.

Choose a good soft English goat's cheese, such as Dorstone or Perroche (both available from Neal's Yard – www.nealsyarddairy.co.uk). Delicious figs are also essential here. The dark Turkish ones are available in September and October.

Lamb cutlets with walnut, fig and goat's cheese salad

1 First you need to marinate the lamb. Take the cutlets, throw the marinade ingredients on and massage them lightly into the meat. Place in a sealed container and refrigerate for at least 4 hours or overnight.

2 Now prepare the sauce. Place all the ingredients in a heavy-based saucepan, stir and put over a medium heat. Bring to the boil, reduce the heat and simmer for 30–40 minutes, until reduced by two-thirds. Remove from the heat and keep somewhere warm.

3 Place the walnuts in a non-stick frying pan and toast over a medium heat for 5 minutes, stirring occasionally. Set aside to cool.

4 To finish the dish, heat up a barbecue or griddle pan until piping hot. Season both sides of the lamb cutlets with salt and pepper. Place on the heat for 3–4 minutes on each side; this will give rare to medium meat. Cook longer if you prefer. Remove the lamb from the grill and leave to rest in a warm place for 2 minutes. While you wait, gently toss together all the salad ingredients, apart from the figs, seasoning with salt and pepper. Make sure the components stay separate and that the cheese doesn't smear the leaves.

5 To serve, put the cutlets on serving plates, pile the salad next to them and the figs alongside. Spoon a scant tablespoon of sauce over each portion of lamb and drizzle a small amount of it over the figs and salad. Serve at once.

serves 4

12 lamb cutlets, French trimmed (you can ask your butcher to do this)
coarse sea salt and black pepper

Marinade
leaves from 6 thyme sprigs, roughly chopped
leaves from 1 rosemary sprig, roughly chopped
2 garlic cloves, crushed
6 tbsp olive oil

Sauce
125ml freshly squeezed orange juice
60ml red wine vinegar
50g honey
1 star anise
1 cinnamon stick

Salad
50g walnuts, broken
100g soft goat's cheese, crumbled
20g mint leaves
25g flat-leaf parsley leaves
2 tbsp olive oil
4 fresh figs, halved or quartered

Kebabs or koftas – Middle Eastern meatballs made with mince and spices – offer endless possibilities for combining flavours and textures. The bread we use here can be replaced with potato, couscous or bulgar wheat. Many alternative herbs and spices also work. Try playing with your favourite ingredients.

Some of our favourite kebabs are served at Al-Waha restaurant in Bayswater and Abu Zaad in Shepherds Bush. They are simply made with minced lamb, grilled over fire, and are always delicious.

The kebabs here are turned fancy by the courgette wrapping. This is more work, so if you prefer to keep it casual you could omit the courgettes. The kebabs can be made in advance up to the stage where you finish them off in the oven. You can then chill them and finish the cooking at the last minute. The sauce can also be chilled and then reheated.

Courgette-wrapped lamb kebabs

serves 2–4

2 tbsp pine nuts
50g stale white bread, crusts removed
300g minced lamb
55g feta cheese, crumbled
1½ tsp ground allspice (pimento)
1 tsp ground cinnamon
¼ tsp ground nutmeg
1 garlic clove, crushed
1 free-range egg
15g flat-leaf parsley, finely chopped
½ tsp salt
½ tsp black pepper
light olive oil for frying, plus a little extra for brushing
2 medium courgettes
salt and pepper

Sauce
2 tbsp olive oil
2 garlic cloves, crushed
400g Italian tinned tomatoes, chopped
a pinch of dried chilli flakes
10 basil leaves

1   Start by making the sauce. Place the olive oil and crushed garlic in a saucepan and stir over a medium heat for 1–2 minutes, just until the garlic cooks lightly. Add the canned tomatoes and season with the chilli flakes and some salt. Bring to the boil, then reduce to a gentle heat and simmer for 25 minutes, until slightly thickened. Remove from the heat, taste and adjust the seasoning. Set aside.

2   Toast the pine nuts in a small, dry frying pan for 4–5 minutes, shaking the pan occasionally, just until they get a little colour. Remove from the heat and leave to cool.

3   Soak the bread in cold water for 2 minutes, then drain and squeeze to remove most of the water. Crumble the bread into a large mixing bowl and add the lamb, crumbled feta, pine nuts, spices, garlic, egg, chopped parsley, salt and pepper. Time to roll up your sleeves and get your hands dirty. Mix all of the ingredients together with your hands until well combined; do not over work the mixture. Shape it into fingers, roughly 10cm by 5cm. There should be 12.

4   Pour a 5mm depth of olive oil into a large frying pan and shallow-fry the kebabs for 1 minute on each side or until they have taken on a nice brown colour. Remove from the pan and set aside on a baking tray.

5   Preheat the oven to 200°C/Gas Mark 6. To prepare the courgettes, use a small knife to slice off both ends and then cut long, thin slices down the length of each courgette (a mandolin will make this job much easier). You will need 12 slices. Brush each slice with a little olive oil and season with salt and pepper. Place a ridged griddle pan over a high heat and leave it there for a few minutes to heat up well. Lay the courgette slices on the hot pan and cook for 2 minutes on each side, so that they get distinctive char marks. Remove to a tray and leave to cool.

6   Wrap each meat finger in a slice of courgette and arrange them in a single layer in a baking dish, seam-side down. Bake in the preheated oven for 8–10 minutes, until cooked through.

7   To serve, bring the sauce back to the boil, tear the basil leaves roughly and stir them in. Arrange the kebabs on serving plates and spoon the sauce over. Drizzle with a little olive oil to finish.

This dish and variations on it, common in Lebanon, Palestine and Syria, make an unusual use of tahini (↗ page xii). Instead of being served cold, the sauce is cooked with the meatballs to give an added boldness and richness. It doesn't look pretty – a problem we solve with the colourful garnish – but the flavours are heavenly. It goes well with Kosheri (↗ page 85) or plain rice.

This is one of Sami's favourites.

Beef and lamb meatballs baked in tahini

serves 4–6

1 First make the tahini sauce. In a bowl, mix together the tahini paste, water, vinegar, garlic and salt. Whisk well until it turns smooth and creamy, with a thick, saucelike consistency. You might need to add some more water. Set the sauce aside while you make the meatballs.

2 Preheat the oven to 200°C/Gas Mark 6. Soak the bread in cold water for 2–3 minutes until it goes soft. Squeeze out most of the water and crumble the bread into a mixing bowl. Add the beef, lamb, garlic, parsley, salt, spices and egg and mix well with your hands.

3 Shape the meat mixture into balls, roughly the size of golf balls. Pour a 5mm depth of light olive oil into a large frying pan. Heat it up, being careful it doesn't get too hot or it will spit all over when frying. Shallow-fry the meatballs in small batches for about 2 minutes, turning them around as you go, until they are uniformly brown on the outside.

4 Put the meatballs on kitchen paper to soak up the oil and then arrange them in a single layer in an ovenproof serving dish. Place in the oven for 5 minutes. Carefully remove from the oven, pour the tahini sauce over and around the meatballs and return to the oven for another 10 minutes. The tahini will take on just a little bit of colour and thicken up; the meatballs should be just cooked through. Transfer to individual plates, garnish liberally with the parsley and lemon zest and serve at once.

35g stale white bread,
  crusts removed
300g minced beef
300g minced lamb
3 garlic cloves, crushed
35g flat-leaf parsley,
  finely chopped
1 tsp salt
½ tsp black pepper
2½ tsp ground allspice (pimento)
1½ tsp ground cinnamon
1 free-range egg
light olive oil for frying
1 tbsp chopped flat-leaf parsley,
  to garnish
grated zest of ½ lemon,
  to garnish

Tahini sauce
150ml tahini paste ↗ page xii
150ml water
70ml white wine vinegar
1 garlic clove, crushed
a pinch of salt

Though there are more flavoursome pieces, the fillet of beef remains a favourite with Ottolenghi customers. Whether it's due to its tenderness or the small amount of visible fat, the fact remains that beef fillet withstood the no-red-meat fad and other fleeting trends to remain one of our biggest sellers. The sauces we choose to accompany it are gutsy and powerful yet not sweet or sour – flavours that can overshadow the fillet.

When buying fillet, you should look for some fat marbling through the meat and ask the butcher to trim off any sinewy bits on the outside. If you require less than a whole fillet, always ask for a piece cut from the centre. This will ensure more even cooking.

Roasted beef fillet (plus three sauces, see opposite)

serves 6–8

1 whole beef fillet, trimmed (around 1.5kg)
3 tbsp olive oil
1½ tsp coarse sea salt
1 tsp black pepper

1   Preheat the oven to 220°C/Gas Mark 7. To get the strong, meaty flavours from the fillet, we start by chargrilling it. Depending on the size of your griddle pan, divide the whole fillet into 2 or 3 pieces that will easily fit in the pan. The head-end piece will be the thickest and therefore will need to cook the longest when it is later put in the oven.

2   After dividing the fillet, place the pieces in a bowl with the oil, salt and pepper and engage in a short massage, rubbing the seasoning into the meat. Place a heavy ridged griddle pan over the highest possible heat and leave for a few minutes, until very hot. Now sear each piece individually, turning it around to get nice dark char marks on all sides; it should take 2–3 minutes in total.

3   Transfer the seared pieces to a roasting tray and put them in the oven to roast. This should take 10–14 minutes for medium-rare, 15–18 minutes for medium or longer for well done. Remember, these are just guidelines. Not all ovens are the same, and neither are fillets, so you should check the meat at different stages. Pressing it with your finger is one option. The more the meat tends to bounce back, the clearer the indication that it is cooked through. If it doesn't, it is still rare. Another option is to stick a sharp knife into the fillet and try to look inside. This is safer but not as elegant. If the knife comes out cold, the meat is definitely not cooked. But keep in mind that the meat will carry on cooking in its own heat after it comes out of the oven.

4   When ready, remove from the oven and leave the fillet in the tray to rest for 10 minutes, then cut it into slices 1–2cm thick. You can also leave it longer and serve at room temperature. Serve with sauce on the side (↗ opposite) .

A Trinidadian recipe from Tricia – red, spicy and full of smoky character. Some like it hot. If you don't, consider reducing the amount of chilli or leaving it out altogether.

Choka (smoky tomato sauce)

1 Place a large, heavy-based frying pan over a high heat and allow it to heat up well. Put the whole tomatoes in it and cook for about 15 minutes, turning them occasionally. The burnt skin will give the sauce its smoky flavour (beware, though; it will take a bit of scrubbing to clean the pan once you're done). Place the hot tomatoes in a bowl and crush them roughly with a wooden spoon. Pick out most of the skin.

2 In a saucepan, heat up the oil well. Remove the pan from the heat while you add the onion so it doesn't spit all over. Return to the heat and cook for 3 minutes on a medium heat just to soften slightly. Add the onion and oil to the crushed tomatoes, together with the chilli, garlic, coriander, paprika and chilli flakes. Taste and season liberally with salt and pepper. Serve warm or at room temperature.

450g plum tomatoes
3 tbsp sunflower oil
1 small onion, thinly sliced
1 mild red chilli, seeded and chopped
2 garlic cloves, crushed
2 tbsp chopped coriander
1 tbsp paprika
a pinch of dried chilli flakes
salt and black pepper

Rocket and horseradish sauce

Put all the ingredients except the yoghurt in a blender or food processor and pulse until smooth. Transfer to a bowl, add the yoghurt and mix well. This sauce will keep for a few days in the fridge in a sealed container.

50g rocket
2 tbsp freshly grated horseradish root
2 garlic cloves, crushed
2 tbsp olive oil
1 tbsp milk
½ tsp salt
½ tsp black pepper
125g Greek yoghurt

Watercress and mustard sauce

Put all the ingredients except the soured cream in a blender or food processor and pulse until smooth. Transfer to a bowl, add the soured cream and mix well. This sauce will keep for a few days in the fridge in a sealed container.

40g watercress
20g wholegrain mustard
1 tbsp Dijon mustard
2 garlic cloves, crushed
2 tbsp olive oil
2 tbsp milk
½ tsp salt
½ tsp black pepper
110ml soured cream

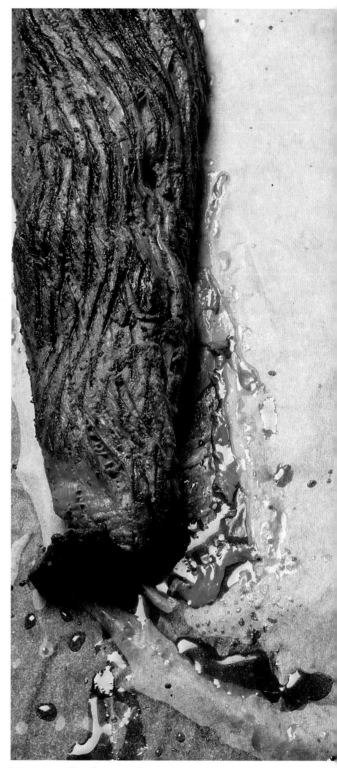

Roasted beef fillet (↗ page 110)

Roast pork belly (↗ page 114)

Scully, the undisputed king of evening service at Ottolenghi Islington, makes the crispest and tastiest pork belly. You enjoy it in two stages: first, when the crackling breaks in your mouth with a crunch, like flaky pastry; second, when the perfectly tender layers of fat and meat melt on your tongue, imparting delectable smoky and herby flavours.

Scully also comes up with the perfect seasonal relishes to go with the pork. Here are two of his creations, but there are infinite other combinations of fruit and spice that we would encourage you to explore. The quantities suggested here will probably leave you with some leftover relish to use later. Serve with anything from mackerel to roast turkey. They should keep in the fridge for at least 10 days, probably longer.

When cooking the pork expect quite a lot of smoke in the kitchen due to the high initial oven temperature. Make sure you keep a window open.

Roast pork belly (plus two relishes, see opposite)

serves 6–8

1 Heat the oven to 250°C/Gas Mark 10 or its highest setting. Place the herbs, garlic and olive oil in a heavy-duty blender or food processor and purée them roughly.

2 Lay the pork belly in an oven tray, skin-side down, and sprinkle lightly with salt and pepper. Use your hands to spread the herb mixture evenly all over the top, pressing it on so it sticks to the meat.

3 Turn the belly skin-side up, wipe the skin dry with kitchen paper and sprinkle sea salt evenly all over the skin (but don't put too much on, as it might create a crust and prevent the crackling forming). Put the tray in the oven and roast for 1 hour, turning the tray around every 20 minutes. Once the skin has formed some crackling, turn the oven down to 170°C/Gas Mark 3, pour the white wine into the tray (avoiding the pork skin) and continue roasting for another hour. If the belly starts turning black, cover it with foil.

4 For the last cooking stage, turn the oven down to 110°C/Gas Mark ¼ and continue roasting for another hour, until the skin has crackled completely and thoroughly dried.

5 Remove the pork from the oven. Use a sharp knife to divide it into segments of a few ribs, cutting between the rib bones. Give as many ribs per portion as the appetite demands. Serve with relish (↗ opposite) on the side.

1 bunch of thyme, roughly chopped
1 bunch of rosemary, roughly chopped
1 head of garlic, cloves peeled and crushed
150ml olive oil
1 piece of pork belly, weighing 2–3kg
1 bottle of white wine
coarse sea salt and black pepper

Gooseberry, ginger and elderflower relish

1 Put the ginger and mustard seeds into a square of muslin, tie it up tightly and put in a heavy-based saucepan. Add the gooseberries, sugar and cordial, stir and place over a very low heat. Simmer gently for an hour, stirring occasionally. You might need to skim off the froth that accumulates on the surface.

2 When ready, the relish should have the consistency of a runny jam. To check this, chill a saucer, put a teaspoonful of the relish on it, then run your finger through it; it should just stay separated but still be slightly runny.

3 Remove the muslin bag, decant the relish into a jar and leave to cool. Either serve straight away with the pork or store in the fridge. It will keep for a week or two.

a small knob of fresh ginger, peeled and thinly sliced
1 tsp mustard seeds
330g gooseberries, trimmed
80g caster sugar
70ml elderflower cordial

Spiced red plum, ginger and rhubarb relish

1 Heat the oven to 150°C/Gas Mark 2. Place the plums and chilli in a heavy-based saucepan and add the cinnamon, star anise, vinegar and half the sugar. Stir well, bring to a light boil and simmer for 20–25 minutes, stirring occasionally and skimming any froth from the surface if necessary. The plums should have a jam-like consistency. To check this, chill a saucer, put a teaspoonful of the chutney on it, then run your finger through it; it should stay separated. Remove from the heat and leave to cool.

2 While the plums are simmering away, place the rhubarb, ginger and remaining sugar in an ovenproof dish. Rub them together with your hands and place in the oven. Cook for 20–30 minutes, stirring from time to time, until the rhubarb is tender. Remove from the oven and leave to cool.

3 Combine the plums and rhubarb and mix well, remove the chilli, then transfer to a jar and leave to cool. Either serve the relish straight away with the pork or store in the fridge, where it will keep for a week or two.

5 red plums (about 240g), stoned and cut into quarters
1 red chilli, halved and seeded
2 cinnamon sticks
1 star anise
100ml red wine vinegar
200g caster sugar
4 stalks of champagne rhubarb (about 200g), cut into 3cm lengths
a small knob of fresh ginger, peeled, very thinly sliced, then cut into tiny strips

There may not be a lot of meat on an oxtail but the long, slow cooking on the bone imparts a magical flavour to this dish. The warm, hearty flavours get a kick of freshness at the end from what the Italians call gremolata – a mixture of parsley, garlic and citrus zest.

Thanks to Nir for the inspiration for this recipe.

Oxtail stew with pumpkin and cinnamon

serves 6

1 Preheat the oven to 180°C/Gas Mark 4. Place a large, heavy-based pan (large enough to accommodate the whole stew later; there will be a lot!) over a high heat and add 2 tablespoons of olive oil. When this is smoking hot, add some of the oxtail pieces and fry on all sides for about 4 minutes, browning the meat well. Make sure you don't sear too many pieces at once or they will boil in their own liquid rather than fry. Transfer the oxtail to a colander and leave to drain off excess fat while you brown the remaining pieces.

2 Remove most of the fat from the pan and add the shallots, carrots and garlic. Return to a medium-high heat and sauté, stirring occasionally, for about 10 minutes, until the vegetables are golden brown.

3 Add the wine to the pan and scrape the base with a wooden spoon to mix in any flavoursome bits left there. Bring to the boil and simmer until it has almost evaporated. Now add the tomatoes. Tie together the thyme and rosemary sprigs with string and drop them in as well, then add the orange zest, bay leaves, cinnamon, star anise, black pepper and some salt. Decant the simmering mixture into a deep baking dish and lay the oxtail pieces on top of the sauce in one layer (keep the pan for later). Cover first with a sheet of baking parchment, placed directly on the oxtail, and then with a tight-fitting lid or a couple of layers of aluminium foil, then place in the oven and bake for 2–3 hours. The meat is ready when it comes easily away from the bone. Lift the oxtail from the sauce, place in a large bowl and leave to cool slightly. If a lot of fat accumulates at the bottom of the bowl, decant some of it using a slotted spoon but keep the rest.

4 When the oxtail is cool enough to handle, pick all the meat from the bones and place back in the large pan. Add the sauce the meat was cooked in, along with the pumpkin cubes and the water. Bring to the boil, then reduce the heat to a gentle simmer and cook for 30 minutes or until the pumpkin is soft. Taste and season the sauce with salt and more black pepper.

5 To make the gremolata garnish for the stew, simply mix the parsley, lemon zest and garlic together. Transfer the stew to a serving bowl and sprinkle the gremolata on top. Serve at once.

olive oil for frying
2kg oxtail pieces
200g shallots, roughly chopped
3 large carrots, roughly chopped
2 garlic cloves, crushed
400ml red wine
650g Italian canned chopped
   tomatoes
10 sprigs of thyme
5 sprigs of rosemary
zest of ½ orange, peeled off
   in long strips
2 bay leaves
2 cinnamon sticks
2 star anise
1 tsp ground black pepper
500g pumpkin or butternut
   squash, peeled, seeded
   and cut into 2.5cm cubes
300ml water
salt

Gremolata
2 tbsp roughly chopped
   flat-leaf parsley
grated zest of 1 large lemon
2 garlic cloves, crushed

Making your own harissa, a key component in Tunisian cooking, is extremely satisfying. The heady, potent paste can be used for flavouring meat and fish, finishing stews, mixing with grilled vegetables – go with it wherever your culinary imagination takes you.

In this recipe, Scully mixes it with yoghurt to get a spicy, smooth marinade in which he leaves the chicken overnight. He normally uses chicken thighs, which are flavoursome and rich. Some supermarkets now offer the thigh meat with bones and skin removed, or you can ask your butcher to bone them for you. If you prefer to use breast meat, skin four breasts and cut them in half widthways, then slice each half horizontally so you get four thin fillets.

Harissa-marinated chicken with red grapefruit salad

1 First make the marinade for the chicken. Over a gas ring or under a very hot grill, toast the red pepper until blackened on the outside. This should typically take about 8 minutes on an open flame, 15–20 minutes under a very hot grill. Place the pepper in a bowl, cover with cling film and leave to cool. Peel the pepper and discard the seeds.

2 Place a dry frying pan on a low heat and lightly toast the coriander, cumin and caraway seeds for 2 minutes. You should be able to smell the aromas of the spices. Transfer them to a pestle and mortar and grind to a powder.

3 Heat the olive oil in a frying pan, add the onion, garlic and fresh and dried chillies and fry over a medium heat for 6–8 minutes, until they turn a dark, smoky colour. Now blitz together all the marinade ingredients except the yoghurt in a food processor or blender; you will have a pure harissa paste.

4 To marinate the chicken, mix the paste with the yoghurt and use your hands to rub it all over the chicken thighs. Layer them in a plastic container, seal and refrigerate overnight.

5 The next day, take each grapefruit and use a small, sharp knife to slice off the top and tail. Now cut down its sides, following its natural lines, to remove the skin and white pith. Over a small bowl, cut in between the membranes to remove the individual segments. Squeeze any remaining juice into a bowl and keep them to make up the 150ml juice required for the sauce.

6 Preheat the oven to 220°C/Gas Mark 7. Lay out the marinated chicken pieces, spaced well apart, on a large baking tray and place in the hot oven. After 5 minutes, reduce the oven temperature to 180°C/ Gas Mark 4 and cook for another 12–15 minutes, until the chicken is almost cooked through. Now place the chicken under a hot grill for 2–3 minutes to give it extra colour and cook it through completely.

7 Meanwhile, place all the sauce ingredients in a small pan and bring to a light simmer. Simmer for about 20 minutes, or until reduced to a third.

8 To serve, toss the rocket and grapefruit segments with the olive oil, salt and pepper. Pile in the centre of 4 serving plates, put the warm chicken on top and drizzle about a tablespoonful of the sauce over each portion.

serves 4

800g organic or free-range chicken thigh meat (about 8–10 thighs)

Harissa marinade
1 red pepper
¼ tsp coriander seeds
¼ tsp cumin seeds
¼ tsp caraway seeds
½ tbsp olive oil
1 small red onion, roughly chopped
3 garlic cloves, roughly chopped
2 mild fresh red chillies, seeded and roughly chopped
1 dried red chilli, seeded and roughly chopped
½ tbsp tomato purée
2 tbsp lemon juice
½ tsp salt
1 tbsp Greek yoghurt

Red grapefruit salad
2 red grapefruit
120g peppery wild rocket
1 tsp olive oil
coarse sea salt and black pepper

Sauce
150ml pink grapefruit juice
130ml lemon juice
150ml maple syrup
¼ tsp salt
a pinch of ground cinnamon
1 star anise

Roast chicken with sumac, za'atar and lemon (↗ page 122)

Roast chicken with saffron, hazelnuts and honey (↗ page 123)

This is a simplified version of the traditional Palestinian dish M'sakhan, where chicken is spiced with sumac and then roasted in the oven over bread. Sumac and za'atar (↗ page xii) that we love and use so much are combined here with fresh lemon to give the chicken a powerful sharp kick. It works fantastically well, and is almost addictive. Try serving with warm pita bread and a garlicky yoghurt sauce, made by mixing Greek yoghurt with crushed garlic, olive oil, salt and pepper.

Roast chicken with sumac, za'atar and lemon

serves 4

1 In a large bowl, mix the chicken with the onions, garlic, olive oil, spices, lemon, stock or water, salt and pepper. Leave in the fridge to marinate for a few hours or overnight.

2 Preheat the oven to 200°C/Gas Mark 6. Transfer the chicken and its marinade to a baking tray large enough to accommodate all the chicken pieces lying flat and spaced apart. They should be skin-side up. Sprinkle the za'atar over the chicken and onions and put the tray in the oven. Roast for 30–40 minutes, until the chicken is coloured and just cooked through.

3 Meanwhile, melt the butter in a small frying pan, add the pine nuts and a pinch of salt and cook over a moderate heat, stirring constantly, until they turn golden. Transfer to a plate lined with kitchen paper to absorb the fat.

4 Transfer the hot chicken and onions to a serving plate and finish with the chopped parsley, pine nuts and a drizzle of olive oil. You can sprinkle on more za'atar and sumac, if you like.

1 large organic or free-range chicken, divided into quarters: breast and wing, leg and thigh
2 red onions, thinly sliced
2 garlic cloves, crushed
4 tbsp olive oil, plus extra for drizzling
1½ tsp ground allspice (pimento)
1 tsp ground cinnamon
1 tbsp sumac ↗ page xii
1 lemon, thinly sliced
200ml chicken stock or water
1½ tsp salt
1 tsp freshly ground black pepper
2 tbsp za'atar ↗ page xii
20g unsalted butter
50g pine nuts
4 tbsp chopped flat-leaf parsley

This dish is inspired by a recipe from Claudia Roden's classic book, *Tamarind and Saffron* (Viking, 1999). It is one of our favourites: it is so easy to make, yet looks stunning, and has the most delicate and exotic combination of flavours (rosewater, saffron and cinnamon), which takes you straight to the famous Jamaa el Fna in Marrakech. Serve with rice or plain couscous.

Roast chicken with saffron, hazelnuts and honey

serves 4

1   In a large bowl, mix the chicken pieces with the onions, olive oil, ginger, cinnamon, saffron, lemon juice, water, salt and pepper. Leave to marinate for at least an hour, or overnight in the fridge.
2   Preheat the oven to 190°C/Gas Mark 5. Spread the hazelnuts out on an oven tray and roast for 10 minutes, until lightly browned. Chop roughly and set aside.
3   Transfer the chicken and marinade to a roasting tray large enough to accommodate everything comfortably. Arrange the chicken pieces skin-side up and put the tray in the oven for about 35 minutes.
4   While the chicken is roasting, mix the honey, rosewater and nuts together to make a rough paste. Remove the chicken from the oven, spoon a generous amount of nut paste on to each piece and spread it to cover. Return to the oven for 5–10 minutes, until the chicken is cooked through and the nuts are golden brown.
5   Transfer the chicken to a serving dish and garnish with the chopped spring onions.

1 large organic or free-range chicken, divided into quarters: breast and wing, leg and thigh
2 onions, roughly chopped
4 tbsp olive oil
1 tsp ground ginger
1 tsp ground cinnamon
a generous pinch of saffron strands
juice of 1 lemon
4 tbsp cold water
2 tsp coarse sea salt
1 tsp black pepper
100g unskinned hazelnuts
70g honey
2 tbsp rosewater ↗ page xii
2 spring onions, roughly chopped

Delicious and nutritious (for once the cliché is utterly true), and also a great way of using up leftover roast chicken. If you happen to have some, skip the roasting part and go straight on to the salad bit.

Shiso leaves are grown in East Asia. We came across them first in one of our favourite Japanese restaurants, Tosa, in Hammersmith. They are from the mint family, taste mildly like cumin and coriander and look a little like stinging nettles. They are available from some Oriental shops but if you can't get them, rocket makes a satisfactory substitute.

Roast chicken and three-rice salad

serves 8

1 Preheat the oven to 220°C/Gas Mark 7. Rub the chicken with 40ml of the olive oil and season liberally with salt and pepper. Place in a roasting tin and put in the oven for 10 minutes. Reduce the temperature to 190°C/Gas Mark 5 and continue to roast for 50–60 minutes, basting with the juices occasionally, until the chicken is thoroughly cooked. Remove from the oven and leave to cool to room temperature. Do not get rid of the cooking juices.

2 While the chicken is roasting, cook the rice. Place the basmati in a saucepan with 400ml of water and a pinch of salt. Bring to the boil, then reduce the heat to minimum, cover and simmer for 20 minutes. Remove from the heat and leave, covered, for 10 minutes. Uncover and leave to cool completely.

3 Place the wild and brown rice in a saucepan and pour in enough cold water to cover the rice by at least 3 times its volume. Bring to the boil and simmer gently, uncovered, for 40–45 minutes, until the rice is tender but still retains a little firmness. If the water runs low, top up with extra boiling water. Drain through a sieve and run under plenty of cold water to stop the cooking. Leave there to drain.

4 Carve the meat from the chicken or simply tear it off in largish chunks. Put it in a bowl large enough to hold the whole salad. In a separate bowl, whisk all the dressing ingredients together with the cooking juices from the chicken. Pour the dressing over the chicken and set aside.

5 Heat the remaining olive oil in a pan, add the onion and a pinch of salt and fry over a medium heat until golden. Remove from the heat and leave to cool.

6 Add the 3 rices, the fried onion and spring onions, chillies and chopped herbs to the chicken. Mix well, then taste and adjust the seasoning.

1 organic or free-range chicken, weighing about 1.5kg
70ml olive oil
200g basmati rice
50g wild rice
50g brown rice
1 onion, thinly sliced
6 spring onions, thinly sliced
4 mild red chillies, seeded and cut into thin strips
50g coriander, chopped
20g mint leaves, chopped
20 shiso leaves, shredded (or rocket)
salt and pepper

Dressing
65ml lemon juice
30ml sesame oil
30ml Thai fish sauce
35ml olive oil

Now you see them, now you don't. That's the fate of these meatballs in our Ledbury Road branch. As soon as we bring them out to the shop they disappear, as if by command of a magician's wand. They are that good!

Turkey and sweetcorn meatballs with roasted pepper sauce

serves 4

1. Preheat the oven to 200°C/Gas Mark 6. To prepare the peppers for the sauce, quarter them with a sharp knife and shave off the white parts and the seeds. Put them in a roasting tray and toss with 2 tablespoons of the olive oil and ½ teaspoon of the salt, then roast in the oven for 35 minutes or until soft. Transfer the hot peppers to a bowl and cover it with cling film. Once they have cooled down a little, you can peel them, although it isn't essential for this sauce. In any case, place them in a blender or food processor with their roasting juices and add the rest of the sauce ingredients. Process until smooth, then taste and adjust the salt if necessary. Set aside.

2. For the meatballs, place a heavy, non-stick frying pan over a high heat and throw in the corn kernels. Toss them in the hot pan for 2–3 minutes, until lightly blackened. Remove and leave to cool.

3. Soak the bread in cold water for a minute, then squeeze well and crumble it into a large bowl. Add all the rest of the ingredients except the sunflower oil and mix well with your hands.

4. Pour a 5mm depth of sunflower oil into your heavy frying pan. Allow it to heat up well and then fry about a teaspoonful of the mince mix in it. Remove, let cool a little and then taste. Adjust the amount of salt and pepper in the uncooked mixture to your liking.

5. With wet hands, shape the mince mix into balls, about the size of golf balls. Cook them in small batches in the hot oil, turning them around in the pan until they are golden brown all over. Transfer to an oven tray, place in the oven at 200°C/Gas Mark 6 and cook for about 5 minutes. When you press one with your finger, the meat should bounce back. If unsure, break one open to check that it is cooked inside. Serve hot or warm, with the pepper sauce on the side.

100g sweetcorn kernels (fresh or frozen)
3 slices of stale white bread, crusts removed
500g minced free-range or organic turkey breast
1 free-range egg
4 spring onions, finely chopped
2 tbsp finely chopped parsley
2½ tsp ground cumin
1½ tsp salt
½ tsp black pepper
1 garlic clove, crushed
sunflower oil for frying

Roasted pepper sauce
4 red peppers
3 tbsp olive oil
1 tsp salt
25g coriander, leaves and stalks
1 garlic clove, peeled
1 small mild chilli, deseeded
2 tbsp sweet chilli sauce
2 tbsp cider vinegar or white wine vinegar

Although turkey is more frequently associated with a sweet red relish, we serve it here with a lemony sauce of herbs and cumin. It is enormously popular around Christmas and Thanksgiving, as it is both traditional and original. The same sauce would work very well with lamb. You can serve this dish either warm or at room temperature.

Marinated turkey breast with cumin, coriander and white wine

serves 4–6

1 Put all the ingredients except the turkey breast in a food processor or blender and process for 1–2 minutes to get a smooth marinade. Put the turkey in a non-metallic container and pour the marinade over it. Massage the marinade into the meat, cover the container and leave in the fridge for 24 hours. Make sure the turkey is immersed in the sauce.

2 Preheat the oven to 220°C/Gas Mark 7. Remove the turkey from the marinade (keep the marinade for later) and put it on a roasting tray. Place in the oven and roast for 15 minutes, then reduce the temperature to 200°C/Gas Mark 6. Continue to cook for 15 minutes, then reduce the temperature again to 180°C/Gas Mark 4. Cook until the turkey is done – another 30–45 minutes. To check, stick a small knife all the way into the centre; it should come out hot. If the meat goes dark before it is ready, cover it with foil.

3 To prepare the sauce, heat up the turkey marinade in a small saucepan and simmer for 15 minutes, until reduced by about half. Taste and season with some more salt and pepper.

4 Remove the turkey from the oven and let it rest for 10 minutes. Slice it thinly and serve with the warm sauce.

5 To serve cold, leave the meat to cool completely and then slice. Adjust the seasoning of the sauce once it is cold and serve on the side.

4 tbsp mint leaves
4 tbsp parsley leaves
4 tbsp coriander leaves
1 garlic clove, peeled
60ml lemon juice
60ml olive oil
125ml white wine
½ tsp ground cumin
½ tsp salt
½ tsp black pepper
½ small organic or free-range turkey breast (about 1kg)

Here is a twist on that out-of-favour classic, duck à l'orange, yet quite far removed from the original. It is spicy and rich, full of intense, multilayered flavours, a recipe you'd always want to return to for some winter comfort.

The English Gressingham duck is the best choice here, as it is bred especially for its larger, more succulent breast. The French Barbary would make a good alternative. Blood oranges are in season throughout the first part of the year but you can easily substitute ordinary oranges.

This dish would go well with a rough mash of orange roots, such as sweet potato, pumpkin or carrot.

Seared duck breasts with blood orange and star anise

serves 4

1 Score the skin of each duck breast in 3 or 4 parallel incisions, without cutting into the meat. Repeat at a 90° angle to the other cuts to get square shaped incisions. Mix the fennel seeds, chilli flakes, cumin, black pepper and salt together, then rub them thoroughly all over the duck breasts with your hands. Place in a bowl, cover with cling film and leave to marinate for a few hours or in the fridge overnight.

2 Using a small, sharp knife, trim off 1cm from the top and bottom of each orange. Standing them up, neatly follow the natural curves of each one with the knife to cut off the skin and white pith. Cut each orange horizontally into roughly 6 slices. Remove the pips, place the slices in a small bowl and set aside.

3 To sear the duck, thoroughly heat a large, heavy frying pan (one for which you have a lid). Place the duck breasts in it, skin-side down, and cook for 3 minutes, until the skin is golden brown and crisp. Turn and cook the other side for 3 minutes, then remove the duck from the pan and keep in a warm place.

4 Discard most of the fat from the frying pan and add the wine, vinegar, orange juice and star anise. Bring to the boil and simmer for 5–6 minutes, until reduced by about half. Taste and add salt and pepper if necessary. Return the duck breasts to the pan and stir to coat them in the sauce. Cover with a lid and simmer gently for 7 minutes.

5 Take the dried chillies, orange slices, plus any extra juice in their bowl, and place carefully next to the duck breasts. Cover again and simmer for another 3 minutes. By this time the meat should be medium-rare.

6 Remove the duck breasts from the sauce, place on a cutting board and leave to rest for 3–4 minutes. While you wait, check the sauce. It may need to be simmered a little longer to thicken it slightly. Taste again and adjust the seasoning if necessary.

7 Slice each breast at an angle into pieces 1cm thick and place on serving plates. Pick the oranges from the sauce and arrange them on the plates with the duck. Pour some of the sauce on top and serve the rest on the side.

4 duck breasts, weighing 180–200g each
2 tbsp fennel seeds
a pinch of dried chilli flakes
2 tsp ground cumin
2 tsp coarsely ground black pepper
1 tsp coarse sea salt
240ml blood orange juice (from about 4 oranges), plus 4 whole blood oranges
180ml red wine
2 tbsp sherry vinegar
16 star anise
6 dried chillies

Another one of Scully's original creations: a warm quail, sweet, piquant and tender, served on a bed of fresh lemony salad spiked with a load of herbs. Perfect for an informal Sunday lunch, especially if the weather is nice and you can barbecue the quail outdoors.

There is a fair amount of preparation involved here but if you start the day before, you'll get the bulk of the work done in advance and also give the birds a longer marinade and a deeper flavour. Make sure you don't get landed with preparing the quail – it's a fiddly and unrewarding job. Instead, ask your butcher to remove the backbone and ribs and spatchcock (flatten, or butterfly) the birds for you.

For information on mograbiah and where to get it, ↗ page 77. Couscous makes an adequate alternative – just follow the cooking instructions on the packet. Dark chicken meat (leg or thigh) could be substituted for the quail.

Barbecued quail with mograbiah salad

1 Start with the marinade. Put all the spices and a pinch of salt in a small food processor bowl or a spice grinder and work them to get a fine, homogenous powder (you could use a pestle and mortar instead, although the mixture won't become as fine). Add the garlic and ginger and continue working to a paste. Transfer the mixture to a large bowl and whisk in the honey and oil until you get a light, uniform mixture. Add the prepared quails, fold back your sleeves and massage the birds intensively with the marinade. Transfer the birds and marinade to a smaller container, then cover and chill for at least 4 hours, preferably overnight.

2 The next day, start by cooking the mograbiah. Bring a litre of water to the boil with a pinch of salt and add the mograbiah. Simmer for 15–18 minutes, until tender but with quite a substantial bite (the cooking time will vary according to the brand, so check the instructions on the packet). Strain into a colander, leave to drain well and then transfer to a bowl. Add the butter and oil, stir well and season with plenty of salt and pepper. Set aside to cool. While you wait, cut the chilli in half lengthways, get rid of the seeds and chop it finely. Finely slice the spring onion. Add them to the cooling mograbiah.

3 To segment the lemon, use a small, sharp knife to trim off 1cm from the top and bottom. Stand it up on a board and neatly follow its natural curves with the knife to take off the skin and all the white pith. Holding the lemon over the bowl of mograbiah, cut along the white membranes encasing the segments to release the segments into the bowl. Squeeze in any remaining juice.

4 To cook the quail, place a griddle pan over a medium heat and leave for a few minutes so it heats up well. Lay the quails on it, spaced well apart, and grill for 10–14 minutes, turning them over half way through. The birds should be just cooked through. Make sure the heat is not too fierce or the birds will darken before they cook through; if this does happen, you could finish them off in a hot oven.

5 When the quail are almost ready, stir the herbs into the mograbiah. Taste and see if you need any more salt, pepper or olive oil.

6 Pile the salad on to serving dishes and place the quail on top, 2 per portion. Serve at once.

serves 4 generously,
or makes 8 tapas-sized portions

**8 large quails, spatchcocked
(see above)**

Marinade
1 tbsp ground cinnamon
2 tbsp ground cumin
10 whole cardamom pods
4 allspice berries (pimento)
1 tbsp ground turmeric
½ tbsp paprika
a pinch of salt
4 garlic cloves, peeled
**2 knobs of fresh ginger
(about 30g), peeled and
coarsely chopped**
2 tbsp honey
180ml olive oil

Salad
125g mograbiah or fregola
↗ page 77
10g unsalted butter
1 tbsp olive oil
1 mild red chilli
1 spring onion
1 lemon
**3 tbsp coarsely chopped
flat-leaf parsley**
**3 tbsp coarsely chopped
coriander**
3 tbsp coarsely chopped mint
coarse sea salt and pepper

You can almost smell the Mediterranean in this salad, with its fresh seafood, herbs, garlic and sumac. The best way to serve it is as part of a mezze selection, with rustic white bread to soak up the juices.

Seafood, fennel and lime salad

serves 4

1 Trim the bases and tops of the fennel bulbs, then slice widthwise as thinly as you can. A mandolin would be useful here. In a large bowl, mix the fennel and red onion with the lime juice and zest, garlic, dill, parsley, chilli, 2 tablespoons of the olive oil and ½ teaspoon of salt. Set aside.

2 Place a heavy cast iron pan, preferably a griddle pan, over a high heat and leave for a few minutes until piping hot. Meanwhile, mix the prawns and squid with the rest of the oil and a pinch of salt. Grill them in small batches, turning them over after 1 minute and continuing until just done (roughly 1 more minute for the squid and 2–3 for the prawns). Transfer to a chopping board and slice the squid into thick rings. You can leave the prawns whole or cut them in half.

3 Add the seafood to the salad bowl and toss together. You can serve immediately or leave it in the fridge for up to 1 day. To serve, stir in the sumac and coriander, then taste and adjust the seasoning. When pomegranate is available, it makes a beautiful garnish.

2 small fennel bulbs,
½ red onion, very thinly sliced
juice and grated zest of 1 lime
2 garlic cloves, crushed
2 tbsp chopped dill
2 tbsp chopped flat-leaf parsley
1 mild chilli, seeded and
 finely chopped
4 tbsp olive oil
8 tiger prawns, peeled
 and de-veined ↗ page 150
350g cleaned baby squid
1 tbsp sumac ↗ page xii
2 tbsp chopped coriander
coarse sea salt
pomegranate seeds,
 to garnish (optional)

Chapter 2 Meat and fish

All the seemingly contradictory flavours come together here surprisingly well to create a harmonious and balanced delicacy. Mackerel, probably our favourite fish, takes the sweetness and the saltiness wonderfully well, producing a light, clean result.

This simple dish relies heavily on the freshness and quality of the ingredients. Mackerel, in particular, is incredible when fresh and inedible when not, so make sure you buy the best.

Grilled mackerel with green olive, celery and raisin salsa

serves 4

1 Stir together all the salsa ingredients. Taste it; it should be sweet, sour and salty. Season with salt and pepper and leave to sit for at least 15 minutes for the flavours to evolve. (At this point, the salsa can be refrigerated for up to 24 hours, if necessary. Before serving, allow it to come to room temperature, refresh with extra chopped parsley and adjust the seasoning.)
2 Set an oven grill to its highest setting. Toss the mackerel fillets gently with the oil and some salt and pepper. Lay the fillets on a flat oven tray, skin side up, and place under the hot grill for 3–4 minutes, or until just cooked.
3 Serve the fish hot or at room temperature, with a spoonful of salsa on top.

**8 mackerel fillets, pin
  bones removed
2 tbsp olive oil
coarse sea salt and black pepper**

Salsa
**125g celery stalks, thinly sliced
60g good-quality green olives,
  stoned and thinly sliced
3 tbsp capers, rinsed
70g good-quality plump raisins
1½ tbsp sherry vinegar
4 tbsp olive oil
3 tbsp honey
15g flat-leaf parsley,
  roughly chopped**

This is definitely a weekend dish – you will need to do a fair amount of preparation a day in advance. Lots of ingredients are involved and a bit of muscle work (even if the process isn't very complicated). Still, what you get is well worth it. First, a small jar of the most astounding spice paste, which you can use to marinate fish and meat (you need only a little of it for this recipe); second, a beautiful fish prepared in minutes on the day; and lastly a round of applause from an impressed crowd.

Tamarind is a sour fruit originating from Asia that comes as a sticky, dark brown pulp. Often the seeds are left in and need to be removed. Also known as the Indian date, it is available in many Asian food shops and some supermarkets.

Thanks, once again, to Scully for this creation.

Grilled mackerel with sweet potato pickle and mint yoghurt

day 1

serves 8 as a starter

8 mackerel fillets, pin bones removed
2 tbsp olive oil
salt and black pepper

1 First make the spice paste. Place a thick-bottomed frying pan over a low heat and spread all the spice paste ingredients out in it apart from the oil. Cook gently for a few minutes, shaking the pan occasionally, until the spices start to release their aroma (do not let them brown or they will taste bitter). Tip everything into a pestle and mortar and pound to a uniform paste. Continue working the spices whilst slowly adding the oil to get a smooth consistency. (You will only need 1 tablespoon of the spice paste for this recipe but the rest can be stored in a clean jar in the fridge for a few months.)

2 Now for the sweet potato pickle. Take the limes and use a small, sharp knife to trim off their tops and tails. Now cut down the sides of the limes, following their natural curves, to remove the skin and all the white pith. Over a small bowl, remove the segments from each lime by slicing between the membranes. Squeeze out any remaining juice over the segments, then discard the membrane.

3 Add the sugar and 1 tablespoon of the spice paste to the lime segments. Stir well to dissolve the sugar, then add the chilli and coriander.

4 Put the sweet potato dice in a pan of boiling salted water and simmer for 3–5 minutes, until they are just cooked but still hold their shape. Drain thoroughly and transfer to a non-metallic bowl. Dress with the lime mixture, leave to cool and then cover with cling film and chill overnight. Remove from the fridge an hour before using.

Spice paste
1½ tbsp cumin seeds
½ tbsp coriander seeds
½ tbsp caraway seeds
½ tbsp fennel seeds
½ cinnamon stick
1 star anise
1 tsp coarse sea salt
1 tsp black peppercorns
3 garlic cloves, crushed
½ red chilli, seeded and roughly chopped
75g fresh ginger, peeled and roughly chopped
150g tamarind paste
100ml vegetable oil

Sweet potato pickle
5 limes
50g caster sugar
½ red chilli, seeded and finely diced
1 tsp chopped coriander
500g sweet potato, peeled and cut into 1cm dice

day 2

5 Start by making the mint yoghurt. Peel the cucumber, cut it in half lengthways and scoop out the seeds with a spoon. Cut the cucumber into 1cm dice and place in a bowl. Add the yoghurt, paprika, lemon juice, mint and oil. Stir well, try a bit and add salt and pepper to taste. Refrigerate until ready to serve.

6 To cook the fish, preheat the grill to its highest setting. Brush the mackerel fillets with the oil and season with salt and pepper. Place the fillets on a baking tray, skin-side up, and put under the grill for 3–4 minutes or until they are cooked through.

7 To serve, place a large spoonful of the pickle on each plate and top with the hot fish. Finish with a little of the mint yoghurt over the fish and serve the rest in a bowl on the side.

Mint yoghurt
1 mini cucumber
225g Greek yoghurt
¾ tsp paprika
juice of ½ lemon
1½ tbsp chopped mint
1½ tbsp olive oil

You can prepare this simple dish in minutes if you make the salsa the day before and store it in the fridge; just remember to let it come back to room temperature before serving. Peeling the peppers is a chore you can choose to avoid if you are feeling lazy. The sauce will not be quite as smooth but it will still taste fantastic.

Organic salmon with red pepper and hazelnut salsa

serves 4

1 First make the salsa. Preheat the oven to 200°C/Gas Mark 6. Quarter the peppers and remove the seeds. Put them in a baking tray and toss with 2 tablespoons of the olive oil and a generous pinch of salt. Roast them in the oven for about 20 minutes, until they are cooked through and slightly charred. Transfer to a bowl, cover with cling film and leave to cool. Keep any of the roasting juices.

2 Roast the hazelnuts on a separate baking tray for 10 minutes, until lightly coloured (you can do this while the peppers are in the oven). Allow them to cool down and then rub with your hands to remove the skins. Chop them roughly.

3 When the peppers are cool, peel them and cut into 5mm dice. Mix with the hazelnuts, the remaining olive oil and all the rest of the salsa ingredients. Taste and add salt and pepper.

4 Put a ridged griddle pan on the highest possible heat and leave for a few minutes. It needs to be very hot! Have an oven tray lined with baking parchment ready. Brush the salmon fillets with the olive oil and sprinkle with salt and pepper. Put them on the hot griddle, skin-side up, and cook for about 3 minutes. Using a fish slice, carefully but briskly remove the fish from the griddle and place them on the lined tray, skin-side down. Be careful not to scrape off the nice char marks when you handle the fish. Bake in the oven for 5–8 minutes, until the fish is just done and very light pink inside. Serve warm, with a generous spoonful of salsa on top.

4 organic salmon fillets, weighing 200g each
2 tbsp olive oil
salt and pepper

Red pepper and hazelnut salsa
2 red peppers
6 tbsp olive oil
15g hazelnuts
15g chives, chopped
1 garlic clove, crushed
juice and grated zest of 1 lemon
2 tbsp cider vinegar

You can prepare both the tuna and the salsa a day in advance and keep them chilled. The salsa will actually improve as its flavours intensify. It will keep for up to 5 days in the fridge. Slice the tuna just before serving it. It is extremely important that the fruit for the salsa is ripe and sweet. Pakistani mangoes, available from May to August, are unrivalled for their sweet flesh and perfumed aroma.

To get more flavour out of the pistachios, you could roast them in the oven at 170°C/Gas Mark 3 for about 8 minutes. If it is the visual effect that you're after, leave them untoasted, as they lose some of their vibrant green colour when baked.

… and yes, we do know that cooked fish should not, under any circumstances, go on a blue chopping board (kitchen hygiene rules). Still, this board had so much history carved into it that Richard, the photographer, insisted on using it for this shot. The poor old board went straight into the bin, taking with it a chunk of history.

Seared tuna with pistachio crust and papaya salsa

serves 6

1   Start with the salsa. Peel the cucumber, halve it lengthways, then scoop out and discard the seeds. Cut it into 1cm dice and put it in a bowl. Add all the rest of the salsa ingredients, stir well and season with salt and pepper. Taste and adjust the seasoning, then chill. It is advisable to allow it to rest for at least an hour for all the flavours to combine.

2   Now for the tuna. Preheat the oven to 250°C/Gas Mark 10, or as high as it will go. Chop the pistachios, preferably in a food processor, until you get fine crumbs. Scatter them on a baking tray and mix with the lemon zest, then set aside.

3   Take the tuna loin and use a sharp knife to divide it along its length into 2 or 3 cylindrical pieces. They should be 6–7cm thick and show the layers of the loin at their ends. Brush the tuna with the olive oil and season with salt and pepper. Place a griddle pan or a heavy cast iron pan over a high heat and leave for a few minutes to heat up. Place the tuna pieces in the pan and sear lightly for 3–4 minutes in total, turning them around as you go. Remove from the pan and leave to cool down a little.

4   Now brush the tuna generously with the mustard and then roll it in the chopped pistachio mixture, using your fingers to cover any bare patches. Place the tuna in a baking tray, transfer to the oven and roast for 5–6 minutes. Check carefully (stick a knife in; it should come out cold), as it might not take that long. What you want is a slightly raw centre with a 1–2cm ring of cooked meat around it. Remove and allow to cool down completely.

5   To serve, cut the tuna into slices 2cm thick. Serve with the salsa on the side or poured on top.

150g shelled pistachio nuts
grated zest of 1 lemon
1kg tuna loin
2 tbsp olive oil
5 tbsp Dijon mustard
coarse sea salt and black pepper

Papaya salsa
1 mini cucumber
1 large, ripe papaya, peeled, seeded and cut into 1cm cubes
1 large, ripe mango, peeled, stoned and cut into 1cm cubes
2 red chillies, seeded and finely chopped
10g fresh ginger, peeled and grated
1 small red onion, finely chopped
grated zest and juice of 2 limes
2 tbsp lemon juice
2 tbsp Thai fish sauce
4 tbsp olive oil
2 tbsp caster sugar

Another incredible recipe from Etti. It is so simple to make, yet the final result is very sophisticated, mixing contrasting textures, colours and temperatures to a faultless harmony. This fresh dish is just right for a warm summer's night, and it doesn't need much more to go with it than a glass of chilled white wine.

Thick, full-fat yoghurt, mixed with some olive oil, can be used instead of labneh. Reduce the amount of chilli if you are not the spicy type.

Pan-fried sea bass on pita with labneh, tomato and preserved lemon

serves 4 as a starter

1 First make the salsa. Score a little shallow cross at the bottom of each tomato and then drop them into boiling water for about 30 seconds. Remove, refresh under plenty of cold water and then peel. Grate them coarsely on a cheese grater and mix with the fresh and dried chilli, herbs and lemon juice. Add salt to taste, then set aside.

2 Remove the flesh of the preserved lemon, discard and slice the skin very finely. Set aside.

3 Now prepare the fish. First, heat the oven to 180°C/Gas Mark 4. Then season the fillets with plenty of salt and pepper. Heat the oil in a non-stick frying pan, large enough to hold all the fillets at once. Add the sea bass and fry, skin-side down, over a medium heat for 3 minutes, until the skin is crisp. Turn the fish over and continue to fry for about 2 minutes, until it is cooked through.

4 While the fish is frying, place the pitas in the oven for 2 minutes, just to warm them up slightly. Put 2 pita quarters on each serving plate and spread a rough, thick layer of labneh over them.

5 Place the hot fish on top of the pitas and spoon some of the salsa over and around the fish. Finish with a few slices of preserved lemon and the pomegranate seeds, if using.

2 wedges of preserved lemon, bought or homemade ↗ page 273
4 sea bass fillets (about 600g in total), pin bones removed, cut in half at an angle
3 tbsp olive oil
2 large pita breads, cut into quarters
120g labneh, bought or homemade ↗ page 272 **at room temperature**
2 tbsp pomegranate seeds (optional)
coarse sea salt and black pepper

Salsa
3 sweet and ripe tomatoes (about 350g in total)
1 mild red chilli, seeded and finely chopped
½ tsp dried chilli flakes
1 tbsp roughly chopped parsley
2 tbsp roughly chopped coriander
50ml lemon juice

This is a quick dish that can be assembled in a flash. The only hard work is getting the seeds out of the pomegranate. And even that isn't so bad (↗ Fennel and feta with pomegranate seeds and sumac, page 17). Have the tahini and seeds ready in advance (but not chilled) and the rest should be done in 10 minutes.

Keep all the pomegranate seeds that you don't use in this dish for the most delectable dessert: buy or make a polenta cake (↗ page 195) and serve warm with crème fraîche that has been lightly scented with rosewater, then sprinkled with pomegranate seeds and broken pistachios.

Pan-fried sea bream with green tahini and pomegranate seeds

serves 4

1 Preheat the oven to 200°C/Gas Mark 6. Line a baking tray with greaseproof paper. Season the fish with plenty of salt and pepper and lay it in the tray, skin-side down. Drizzle with the olive oil and then bake for 6–7 minutes. The fish should be firm and 'bounce' back when you poke it with a finger.
2 Place the fish on serving plates and spoon the tahini sauce generously on top. Garnish with the chopped parsley, lemon zest and pomegranate seeds. Place a lemon wedge next to the fish and serve at once.

4 sea bream fillets, scaled and pin bones removed
4 tbsp olive oil
½ quantity of Green tahini sauce ↗ page 272 **at room temperature**
2 tbsp roughly chopped flat-leaf parsley
grated zest of 1 lemon
100g pomegranate seeds (about ½ pomegranate)
coarse sea salt and pepper
4 lemon wedges, to serve (optional)

We encourage you to be cunning. Many people think they don't like sardines, associating them with tins, bones and a mess in the kitchen. Make this sweet and sour delicacy, however, and we guarantee you will convert a few vehement sardinophobes.

Ask your fishmonger to scale, bone and butterfly the sardines, leaving the tails on. It is practically impossible to do this at home. You could replace the sardines with mackerel fillets, cooking them for a couple of minutes longer.

Sardines stuffed with bulgar, currants and pistachios

serves 4

1   Start with some preparations for the stuffing. Put the bulgar in a bowl, cover it with cold water and leave to soak for 15–20 minutes, until soft. Drain in a fine sieve and squeeze to remove excess moisture. Return to the bowl.
2   In a separate bowl, cover the currants with a little warm water and leave to soak for 5 minutes, then drain.
3   Heat the oven to 150°C/Gas Mark 2. Sprinkle the pistachios over a baking tray and roast in the oven for 10 minutes, until lightly coloured. Leave to cool and then chop roughly.
4   Now add the drained currants and the pistachios to the bulgar, together with the lemon zest, juice and chopped parsley (reserving a little parsley to garnish). Stir in the spices, mint, garlic, molasses, sugar and 5 tablespoons of olive oil, then season with salt and pepper to taste.
5   In a separate bowl, mix the prepared sardines with the remaining olive oil and season with a little salt and pepper.
6   Heat the oven to 180°C/Gas Mark 4. To stuff the sardines, lay them out on a chopping board, skin-side down, with the tail facing away from you. Spoon a little bit of the bulgar stuffing in the middle of each fish and fold first the head end over the stuffing and then the tail to form a roll. Carefully push a wooden cocktail stick down through the fish, catching both sides of the fillets. The tail should slightly stick up in the air. Gently press back any mix that is escaping from the sides.
7   Arrange the sardines on a baking tray lined with baking parchment, place in the oven and roast for 5–6 minutes, until just cooked through. Serve hot or at room temperature, accompanied by the lemon wedges and garnished with a little chopped parsley.

100g medium bulgar wheat
30g currants
30g pistachio nuts
grated zest of 1 lemon
40ml lemon juice
2 tbsp chopped flat-leaf parsley
½ tsp ground cinnamon
1 tsp ground allspice (pimento)
3 tbsp dried mint
2 garlic cloves, crushed
2 tbsp pomegranate molasses
   ↗ page xii
1 tsp caster sugar
6 tbsp olive oil
8 fresh sardines, scaled, boned and butterflied (see above)
salt and black pepper
4 lemon wedges, to serve

Delicate yet exploding with flavour, this is a Scully classic that always seems to come back to our evening menu in Islington. The saffron potato and the aioli offer a mild, creamy base against which the scallops shine, while the asparagus and samphire bring freshness and an added taste of the sea.

Saffron is expensive but a little of it goes a long way, and it does impart the most incredible shade of red and a magnificent aroma. There is a lot of poor-quality saffron around, so look out for particular types, such as the Italian Aquila or the milder but still good Spanish Superior.

The British scallop season is from August to December. Choose hand-dived where possible and look for plump, creamy-coloured ones.

Fried scallops with saffron potatoes, asparagus and samphire

serves 4 as a starter

1 First make the aioli. Preheat the oven to 150°C/Gas Mark 2. Place the garlic cloves on a sheet of aluminium foil, drizzle with a little olive oil and sprinkle with a pinch of salt. Wrap in the foil to seal and then roast in the oven for 25–35 minutes, until very tender. Remove from the oven and leave to cool, then mash with a fork.

2 Mix together the olive oil and sunflower oil. In a mixing bowl, combine the egg yolk, vinegar, mustard, garlic, salt and a good grind of black pepper. Whisk constantly by hand or in a food processor while slowly trickling in the oils. At the end, the aioli should be thick, like a mayonnaise (you might need a little more or a little less oil). Taste it and see if you want to add any more salt and pepper.

3 Put the potatoes in a medium saucepan, cover with cold water, then add the saffron and a generous pinch of salt. Bring to the boil, reduce the heat and simmer for 6–8 minutes; the potatoes should still be slightly firm. Drain and leave in a cool place.

4 While the potatoes are cooking, cut the tomato into 4 wedges and use a small, sharp knife to remove the seeds. Cut each quarter into 5mm dice and set aside.

5 Wash the samphire in plenty of water and then throw it into a pan of boiling water. Leave for just 1 minute, then use a slotted spoon to lift it from the pan and into a colander. Refresh under cold running water and set aside.

6 Trim the woody ends of the asparagus and cut each spear into 3cm lengths. Drop into the pan of boiling water the samphire was cooked in, simmer for 2–3 minutes, then drain at once into a colander and run under plenty of cold water. Set aside to dry.

7 To serve, heat up 2 large frying pans with half the olive oil in each. When piping hot, add the potatoes to one of the pans. Toss them for a minute or two to get some colour and then add the asparagus and samphire just to warm them up. Taste and season.

8 At the same time, season the scallops liberally with salt and pepper and put them into the other pan. Sear them for 30–50 seconds on each side or until just cooked (this will depend on their size).

9 Straight away, divide the warm scallops and vegetables between small serving plates or the scallop shells and spoon about a teaspoon of the aioli on top of each portion (the leftover aioli will keep in the fridge for 2 days and can be used in sandwiches or for dressing fish). Garnish with the diced tomato and a drizzle of olive oil and serve at once.

400g Desiree potatoes, peeled and cut into 1cm dice
a large pinch of saffron strands
1 small tomato
40g samphire
8 medium asparagus spears
4 tbsp olive oil
8 medium-large fresh scallops, trimmed
4 scallop shells, washed (optional)
coarse sea salt and black pepper

Aioli
7 garlic cloves, peeled
100ml olive oil, plus a little extra for roasting the garlic
50ml sunflower oil
1 free-range egg yolk
1½ tsp white wine vinegar
¼ tsp Dijon mustard
¼ tsp fine sea salt

This is another one of Etti's masterpieces. There is no other way to describe it. Two of our recipe testers for this book, Claudine Boulstridge and Philippa Shepherd, both said that it is now their favourite, because it is dead easy and utterly delicious. The flavour of the Arak, a Middle Eastern liquor made from aniseed and distilled grapes, complements but also mellows the intensity of the tomato and olives, coating the prawns in a heavenly buttery sauce.

This dish needs to be served as soon as it is made, accompanied by pieces of wholesome bread to soak up the sauce.

Buttered prawns with tomato, olives and Arak

serves 4 as a starter

4 plum tomatoes
12 tiger or king prawns
50g softened unsalted butter
½ tsp dried chilli flakes
50g Kalamata olives, stoned
20ml Arak (or Pernod)
3 garlic cloves, very thinly sliced
2 tbsp chopped flat-leaf parsley
coarse sea salt

1 Start by preparing the tomatoes. Make a tiny shallow cross with a sharp knife at the bottom of each one and put them in boiling water for 30 seconds. Remove, refresh under plenty of cold water, then drain. Now peel the skin away and cut each tomato into 4–6 wedges. Set aside.
2 To prepare the prawns, peel the shells away from the bodies, keeping the tail segment of the shell on. Cut a shallow slit along the back of each prawn and remove the dark vein using the tip of a small knife.
3 Place a frying pan over a high heat. When very hot, add 20g of the butter and sauté the prawns quickly for 2 minutes, shaking the pan as you go. Add the tomatoes, chilli and olives and cook for another 2–3 minutes, until the prawns are nearly cooked through. Add the Arak carefully (it tends to catch fire!). Let the alcohol evaporate for a minute before quickly adding the remaining butter plus the garlic, parsley and some salt. Toss for a second for everything to come together in a runny sauce, then serve immediately, with bread.

Baking and patisserie

This bread is very easy to make and needs nothing more than some good cheese or cured meat to go with it. The combination of the buckwheat flour and walnuts gives it its unique earthy depth. Thanks to Jim again.

Sour cherry and walnut stick

1 Put the water and yeast in the bowl of an electric mixer, stir together and leave to stand for 10 minutes. Add the orange juice, mix again and then add both types of flour. Set the machine on a low speed and knead for 5 minutes with the dough hook until everything comes together in a rough ball.

2 Stop the machine and scrape the dough from the bottom of the bowl. Add the salt, turn up to a high speed and work for 4 minutes, by which time the dough should be smoother and have a silky texture. Stop the mixer, add the cherries and walnuts and mix on a medium speed for another minute.

3 Turn the dough out on to a lightly floured work surface and knead by hand, turning it as you do so, until all the cherries and walnuts have disappeared inside the dough and it appears smooth. Shape the dough into a ball and put it in a large bowl. Cover with a damp cloth and leave in a warm place for 1½ hours or until the dough has doubled in volume.

4 Turn the risen dough out on to a floured surface. Trying not to beat too much air out of it, pull the edges of the dough so that they all meet at the centre top to form a puffed, round cushion shape. Use a long object such as the handle of a wooden spoon to divide the dough into 2 equal spheres. Press down a little and then fold one half over the other. Crimp the round edges together with your fingers to seal them as if you were making a Cornish pasty. Now roll this on the floured surface to create a torpedo-like baguette shape. Lay it gently on a floured tea towel, cover loosely with cling film and leave to rise in a warm place for another 45 minutes.

5 Heat the oven to 220°C/Gas Mark 7 and put a small, shallow pan of hot water in the bottom. Once the dough has risen by about 50 per cent, roll it off the cloth and on to a baking sheet. Be careful not to shake it too much or to press hard, so as not to lose air. Use a very sharp non-serrated knife to make 3 diagonal slashes, 1cm deep, on top of the bread (an old-fashioned razor blade is best for this job).

6 Place the tray in the oven and bake for 20–25 minutes. Check if the bread is ready by tapping on its base; it should sound hollow. Leave to cool on a wire rack.

160ml lukewarm water (not more than 30°C)
1½ tsp active dried yeast or 2¼ tsp (tightly packed) fresh yeast
40ml orange juice
250g country brown flour (Allinson's country grain brown bread flour or Hovis granary flour), plus extra for dusting
65g buckwheat flour
1 tsp salt
50g dried sour cherries
50g walnuts, roughly broken into pieces

Top to bottom: Green olive loaf (↗ page 163), Sour cherry and walnut stick (↗ page opposite), Crusty white Italian loaf (↗ page 162)

Soft, rich and chewy, focaccia is our favourite when sipping a glass of wine before a meal. It is perfect with crumbly mature Parmesan. Jim Webb, who tried the book's sweet and baking recipes and played a huge part in their creation, always emphasises the importance of not overdoing the topping. Focaccia isn't a fat pizza but a bread, enriched with oil and some flavouring. Just make sure to use the best olive oil and be generous with it.

The grape focaccia might seem unusual but it goes wonderfully well with cheese. Try it with a mature Taleggio. Or, since the oil gives focaccia a prolonged life, have it the next day for breakfast, like a good Danish pastry.

Focaccia (plus three toppings)

1 For the starter, put the yeast and water in a large mixing bowl and stir with a wooden spoon until the yeast dissolves. Add the flour and stir until you get a porridge-like consistency. Cover the bowl with a damp cloth and leave somewhere warm for about 2 hours, until doubled in size.

2 In a mixer fitted with a dough hook attachment, mix the starter with the flour, sugar and olive oil. Knead on a low speed for 6 minutes, then add the salt and work on a fast speed for 2 minutes.

3 Brush a large bowl with oil, place the dough in it and brush the surface of the dough with more oil. Cover the bowl with a damp cloth and leave in a warm place for 1 hour, until the dough has doubled in size.

4 Turn the dough on to a floured work surface and stretch and flatten it into a rectangle. Try not to work it too much. Take one of the short edges of the rectangle and fold it into the centre. Take the other end and fold it over the first one to form 3 layers of dough.

5 Take a heavy baking tray, roughly 30 × 40cm, and brush it with oil. Lift the dough on to the tray, placing it so the seam is at the bottom, and flatten it by pressing hard with your fingers. Cover with cling film and leave to rise for another hour. During this time you will need to work on the dough 3 or 4 times. Press it down with your fingertips and stretch it out gently to the edges of the baking tray each time. By the end of this process it should cover the whole tray in a layer about 2cm thick and have lots of bumps and little hills in it.

6 Preheat the oven to 220°C/Gas Mark 7. Follow one of the topping instructions opposite. Place the focaccia in the oven and bake for 10 minutes, then reduce the temperature to 190°C/Gas Mark 5 and continue for 15–20 minutes. Check underneath the bread to make sure it is baked through. When it is out of the oven and still hot, brush with plenty of olive oil.

330g strong white bread flour
1 tbsp light brown sugar
**2 tbsp olive oil, plus extra
  for brushing**
1 tbsp coarse sea salt

Starter
**1½ tsp active dried yeast
  (or 15g fresh yeast)**
**420ml bottled still spring
  water, lukewarm**
330g strong white bread flour

Parsley and olive topping

Stir together the olive oil, garlic and parsley. Dot them over the top of the dough. Spread the pitted olives over it, pressing them into the dough, and sprinkle with salt.

2 tbsp olive oil
1 garlic clove, crushed
30g flat-leaf parsley, chopped
50g kalamata olives, pitted
coarse sea salt

Grape and fennel seed topping

Halve the grapes lengthwise. Mix the sugar and fennel seeds together. Stud the top of the dough with the grapes and sprinkle with the sugar and seeds.

300g seedless red grapes
50g caster sugar
2 tsp fennel seeds

Red onion and goat's cheese topping

Mix the onion with the olive oil and scatter it on top of the bread. Dot with pieces of crumbled goat's cheese and sprinkle with a little salt.

1 small red onion, thinly sliced
2 tbsp olive oil
100g goat's cheese, crumbled
coarse sea salt

We don't miss an opportunity to sing the praises of Swiss chard –
a very popular green where we come from but not so easily found here.
Its acidic aroma, with strong earthy notes, enhances the similar qualities
of the Jerusalem artichoke. The added creamy texture here guarantees
you'll want to make this tart again and again.

Jerusalem artichoke and Swiss chard tart

serves 4–6

1 Lightly oil a 22–24cm loose-bottomed tart tin. On a lightly floured
   surface, roll out the pastry to 2–3mm thick. Use the pastry to line
   the tin, pressing it well into the corners and the sides and allowing
   it to spill over the edge by at least 2cm. This excess will be trimmed
   later. Prick the base with a fork in a few places, then leave the tart
   case to rest in the fridge for at least half an hour.

2 Heat the oven to 170°C/Gas Mark 3. Cut a circle of greaseproof paper
   greater in diameter than the base plus the sides of the tart tin. Tuck
   it in the pastry case and fill up with dried beans or rice. Bake the case
   blind for 35 minutes, then remove the paper and the beans or rice
   (you can keep them and reuse indefinitely for baking blind). Return
   the pastry case to the oven and bake for a further 5–10 minutes,
   until light golden and thoroughly cooked. Remove from the oven
   and leave to cool.

3 While your pastry is resting and baking, prepare the filling. Place
   the artichokes in a saucepan, cover with cold water and bring to
   the boil with a little salt. Reduce the heat and simmer for 15 minutes,
   until tender. Drain and leave to cool.

4 Cut the chard leaves off the stalks, then roughly chop the leaves
   and stalks, keeping them separate. Heat the oil in a large frying pan,
   add the stalks and fry for 2 minutes, then add the leaves and the
   rosemary. Sauté for 6–8 minutes, depending on how woody the chard
   is. It should wilt completely. Remove from the heat, stir in the lemon
   juice, garlic and some seasoning and leave to cool.

5 Whisk together the double cream, crème fraîche, eggs and a pinch
   of salt and pepper. Spread the artichokes, chard and feta over the
   base of the pastry case, arranging them so that all the ingredients
   are visible. Pour the custard mixture on top. Make sure that you
   don't fill the tart to the rim, so that bits of the filling still show above
   the custard. Carefully transfer the tart to the hot oven and bake
   for 15 minutes. Then cover with foil, keeping it away from the tart's
   surface, and bake for a further 45 minutes, until the filling is set.
   If the top is still pale at this point, remove the foil and leave the tart
   in the oven for a few extra minutes.

6 Take out of the oven and allow to cool slightly. Break off the
   excess pastry and take the tart out of the tin. Serve warm or at
   room temperature.

Filling

1 quantity of Shortcrust pastry
↗ page 281 or use 500g bought
   pastry
vegetable oil for brushing the tin

Filling
600g Jerusalem artichokes,
   peeled and cut into 2cm cubes
250g Swiss chard (or spinach)
4 tbsp olive oil
½ tsp chopped rosemary
juice of ½ lemon
1 garlic clove, crushed
220ml double cream
50ml crème fraîche
2 medium free-range eggs
150g feta cheese, broken
   into pieces
salt and pepper

Top to bottom: Sweet and spicy beef and pork pie (↗ page 174), Jerusalem artichoke and Swiss chard tart (↗ opposite)

This is not your usual meat pie. It is rich, sweet and spicy, and looks impressive yet rustic when served whole at the table. Take it on a picnic or serve warm with a salad of mixed bitter leaves.

Sweet and spicy beef and pork pie

serves 6–8

1. Lightly oil a 22–24cm loose-bottomed tart tin. On a lightly floured surface, roll out the pastry to 2–3mm thick. Use the pastry to line the tin, pressing it well into the corners and the sides and allowing it to spill over the edge by at least 2cm. This excess will be trimmed later. Prick the base with a fork in a few places, then leave the tart case to rest in the fridge for at least half an hour.

2. Heat the oven to 170°C/Gas Mark 3. Cut a circle of greaseproof paper greater in diameter than the base plus the sides of the tart tin. Tuck it in the pastry case and fill up with dried beans or rice. Bake the case blind for 35 minutes, then remove the paper and the beans or rice (you can keep them and reuse indefinitely for baking blind). Return the pastry case to the oven and bake for a further 5–10 minutes, until light golden and thoroughly cooked. Remove from the oven and leave to cool.

3. You can toast the pine nuts for the filling at the same time as cooking the pastry case. Scatter them on a baking tray and leave in the oven for 8 minutes or until they go golden.

4. To make the filling, heat half the olive oil in a large, heavy saucepan, add the beef and break it down with a fork. Cook over a high heat for a few minutes, until coloured. Add the sausage meat, mix well with your fork and keep on cooking over a medium heat for 15 minutes or until golden. Stir in the tomato purée and sugar and cook for another 3 minutes. Then add the salt, pepper, mint and all the spices and cook for 10 minutes over a low heat.

5. In the meantime, fry the onions in the remaining olive oil in a separate pan for about 10 minutes, until golden brown. Drain off most of the oil and add the onions to the cooked meat. Add the pine nuts and taste for salt and pepper.

6. Heat the oven to 190°C/Gas Mark 5. To assemble the tart, spoon half the hot meat mixture into the pastry case. Make 3 shallow holes in the mixture, then break 3 eggs, one by one, and pour them into the holes. Using a wooden spoon, stir the eggs gently in the meat – just enough to disperse them a little, while keeping areas with more egg and maintaining some distinction between white and yolk. Spoon the rest of the meat on top, create some holes in it and break in the rest of the eggs, dispersing them as before.

7. Put the pie in the oven and bake for about 15 minutes, until the eggs are set. If the top begins to darken too much, cover it with foil for the remaining cooking period.

8. Remove from the oven and break off the excess pastry with your hands. Take the pie out of the tin and serve hot or warm, garnished with the parsley.

1 quantity of Shortcrust pastry
↗ page 281 **or use 500g bought pastry**
vegetable oil for brushing the tin

Filling
50g pine nuts
8 tbsp olive oil
400g minced beef
400g sausage meat
3 tbsp tomato purée
2 tsp sugar
2 tsp salt
1 tsp coarsely ground black pepper
1 tbsp dried mint
2 tsp ground allspice (pimento)
1 tsp ground cinnamon
½ tsp ground nutmeg
1 tsp sweet paprika
½ tsp cayenne pepper or dried chilli flakes
2 onions, thinly sliced
7 free-range eggs
2 tbsp chopped flat-leaf parsley

These sweet and savoury tarts are best served warm, or even at room temperature, definitely not piping hot. The tart sweetness of the carrot relish and the savoury taste of the goat's cheese are a spectacular match (made in Scully's always creative mind).

Butternut, carrot and goat's cheese tartlets

makes 6

1 Start by making the pastry. Sift the flour into a large bowl and add the salt and poppy seeds. Rub the butter into the flour with your fingertips, until the mixture resembles fine breadcrumbs. Add the milk and stir until the mixture just starts to form a ball. Do not mix any more. Shape the dough into a fat disc, wrap in cling film and chill for a few hours.

2 Preheat the oven to 170°C/Gas Mark 3. Mix the diced squash with 1 tablespoon of the olive oil and some salt and pepper. Put the squash into a roasting dish and cook in the oven for 15 minutes or until semi-soft. Leave to the side to cool down.

3 While the squash is cooking, heat the remaining oil in a large saucepan and add the mustard seeds. Cook until they start to pop, then add the grated carrots and cook, stirring frequently, for 10 minutes. Stir in the sugar, white wine vinegar and orange juice, bring to the boil and then reduce the heat to a low simmer. Cook for 20–25 minutes, stirring occasionally, until almost all the liquid has evaporated. Remove from the heat and leave to cool.

4 Take 6 tartlet tins, 10cm in diameter and 2cm deep, and brush them lightly with the melted butter. On a lightly floured work surface, roll out the pastry to 3–4mm thick. Cut out circles big enough to line the tins and gently press them into each one, working with your fingers around the edges to line them evenly. Cut off any excess pastry, then chill the tartlet cases for at least 30 minutes. Line the base and sides of each one with a disc of greaseproof paper and fill it with baking beans or rice. Bake blind at 170°C/Gas Mark 3 for 20 minutes, then remove the paper and beans or rice and return to the oven for 5–10 minutes, until golden brown. Leave to cool.

5 Turn the oven up to 180°C/Gas Mark 4. In a large bowl, combine the egg yolk with the cream, chives, grated Parmesan, a pinch of salt and a good grind of black pepper. Whisk together until the cream firms up to form soft peaks and then refrigerate.

6 To assemble the tartlets, divide the carrot mixture equally between the pastry cases, spreading it over the bases. Top with the butternut squash and crumble the goat's cheese over it. Place the tartlets on a baking tray and spoon over the cream mixture, filling them almost to the top. Place in the oven and bake for 8–10 minutes, until the filling is golden and set. Once the tarts are cool enough to handle, remove them from their tins. Serve warm, with a peppery salad.

450g (net weight) peeled and seeded butternut squash, cut into 2cm dice
2 tbsp olive oil
1 tsp mustard seeds
180g (net weight) peeled and coarsely grated carrots
35g caster sugar
30ml white wine vinegar
50ml orange juice
30g unsalted butter, melted
150g goat's cheese
1 free-range egg yolk
120ml whipping cream
20g chopped chives
40g Parmesan cheese, freshly grated
salt and black pepper

Pastry
230g plain flour
½ tsp salt
25g poppy seeds
110g cold butter, cut into small pieces
60ml milk

Of all the yeasted products, brioche is probably the easiest to make at home and extremely worth your while. It is deliciously buttery and has a smooth, light texture. When just out of the oven, it almost feels as if you are eating air.

You need to make the brioche dough a day in advance, as it requires a slow proving process in the fridge. This will give it a deeper flavour and smoother texture. The method requires a freestanding electric mixer with a dough hook attachment. A beater attachment will also work. Don't attempt to use a whisk!

The quantity of brioche dough given below makes a small loaf, which you can serve for breakfast with (even) more butter and jam, or use to make a sinful French toast, accompanied by Mascarpone cream (↗ page 278) and maple syrup. Alternatively use the dough as the base for some little 'pizzas' (↗ page 178) or to make a sweet galette (↗ page 264).

Brioche

makes 1 × 500g loaf

1 Place the lukewarm water and yeast in the bowl of an electric mixer. If using dried yeast, leave for 10 minutes for the yeast to activate. Gently stir with your finger until the yeast dissolves. Add all the rest of the ingredients apart from the butter and start working them together with a spatula until the flour is incorporated.

2 Attach the bowl to the machine and work on a low speed for about 3 minutes. The dough should become smooth but will still stick to the bowl. Once it has reached this stage, scrape it off the sides of the bowl, increase the speed of the machine to medium-high and start adding the diced butter. Do this gradually, making sure that the butter is more or less incorporated into the dough before adding more. Once all the butter is in, keep the machine working until the dough is shiny, has no lumps of butter and comes away naturally from the sides of the bowl. This will take about 9 minutes, depending on your machine (the dough will be lukewarm; make sure it doesn't get hot). Once or twice during the mixing process, you might need to stop the machine, scrape the sides of the bowl clean and very(!) lightly dust with flour.

3 Remove the dough from the mixer and place in a lightly greased bowl or plastic container that is about twice as large as the dough. Cover with cling film and leave at room temperature for 1 hour. Then transfer to the fridge and leave for 14–24 hours before using. During this time, the dough will not rise much or change significantly.

4 Have ready a 500g loaf tin, lightly brushed with some melted butter. Take the dough out of the fridge, place it on a work surface and dust very lightly with flour. Using your hands, knock the dough down and then shape it into a rectangle that is about the size of the tin base. Place it inside the tin, cover with cling film and leave somewhere warm for 2–3 hours, until almost doubled in height.

5 Preheat the oven to 170°C/Gas Mark 3. Brush the dough lightly with beaten egg. Put the tin on an oven tray and place in the hot oven. After about 15 minutes, the loaf should be dark brown and baked through. Stick a skewer inside to make sure it is completely dry. Remove from the oven and leave until cool enough to handle, then take out of the tin and leave to cool completely.

2 tbsp lukewarm water (not more than 30°C)
1 tsp active dried yeast or 1½ tsp (tightly packed) fresh yeast
190g strong white bread flour, plus extra for dusting
½ tsp salt
20g caster sugar
2 medium free-range eggs, at room temperature, plus 1 egg, beaten, to glaze the loaf
75g cold unsalted butter, cut into 2cm dice, plus extra melted butter for brushing the tin

Hardly a pizza (but we couldn't think of a more suitable name), this is the ultimate comfort snack. The buttery, slightly sweet brioche makes a superior base for the salty feta and sweet and sour tomatoes.

'Pizza' with feta, tomato and olives

1   Put the brioche dough on a lightly floured work surface and roll it out to a sheet about 2cm thick. Using a pastry cutter or the rim of a large cup, cut out 6 circles, 9–10cm in diameter. Place on a non-stick baking tray and leave to rise for 1–2 hours, depending on how warm the kitchen is. The brioche discs should double in height.

2   While the brioche is rising, prepare the toppings. Cut the tomatoes into quarters lengthways and then cut each quarter into 2 long pieces. Place the wedges skin-side down on a baking tray and drizzle over the oil and vinegar. Sprinkle the salt, pepper and mint on top. Put in the oven for up to an hour, until the tomatoes have dried out but still retain some moisture. Leave to cool.

3   For the caramelised onion, put the onion, oil, sugar and salt in a large pan and cook for 7 minutes over a high heat, stirring occasionally, until golden. Remove from the heat and stir in the crushed garlic. Leave to cool.

4   Preheat the oven to 170°C/Gas Mark 3. To assemble the brioche pizzas, brush the risen dough discs with a little beaten egg and place a generous amount of the caramelised onion in the centre. Top with lots of tomatoes, feta and olives. Remember, the size of the dough will increase substantially in the oven, so be generous! Drizzle with a little olive oil and season with salt and pepper. Bake for 15–20 minutes. Check the bottoms of the pastries to make sure they are thoroughly cooked.

5   Remove from the oven and leave to cool. Lightly brush with more olive oil and garnish with the parsley leaves.

makes 6 snack-sized pizzas

1 quantity of Brioche dough
↗ page 177
1 free-range egg, lightly beaten
75g feta cheese, crumbled
40g Kalamata olives, pitted
olive oil for drizzling
6 parsley leaves, to garnish
coarse sea salt and black pepper

Oven-dried tomatoes
300g plum tomatoes
1 tsp olive oil
1 tsp balsamic vinegar
½ tsp coarse sea salt
¼ tsp black pepper
½ tsp dried mint

Caramelised onion
1 onion, thinly sliced
1 tbsp olive oil
¼ tsp sugar
¼ tsp salt
1 garlic clove, crushed

Spicy, sweet and punchy, baked fresh and served warm, this is the sort of starter that can precede almost anything. The generous soured-cream base and the lightness of the puff pastry carry the sweet potato easily without the risk of a carb overdose. Serve with a plain green salad.

Sweet potato galettes

makes 4

1 Preheat the oven to 200°C/Gas Mark 6. Bake the sweet potatoes in their skins for 35–45 minutes, until they soften up but are still slightly raw in the centre (check by inserting a small knife). Leave until cool enough to handle, then peel and cut into slices 3mm thick.

2 While the sweet potatoes are in the oven, roll out the puff pastry to about 2mm thick on a lightly floured work surface. Cut out four 7 × 14cm rectangles and prick them all over with a fork. Line a small baking sheet with baking parchment, place the pastry rectangles on it, well spaced apart, and leave to rest in the fridge for at least half an hour.

3 Remove the pastry from the fridge and brush lightly with beaten egg. Using a palette knife, spread a thin layer of soured cream on the pastries, leaving a 5mm border all round. Arrange the potato slices on the pastry, slightly overlapping, keeping the border clear. Season with salt and pepper, crumble the goat cheese on top and sprinkle with the pumpkin seeds and chilli. Bake for 20–25 minutes or until the pastry is cooked through. Check underneath; it should be golden brown.

4 Whilst the galettes are cooking, stir together the olive oil, garlic, parsley and a pinch of salt. As soon as the pastries come out of the oven, brush them with this mixture. Serve warm or at room temperature.

3 sweet potatoes, weighing about 350g each
250g puff pastry, or use ½ quantity of the Rough puff pastry ↗ page 280
1 free-range egg, lightly beaten
100ml soured cream
100g hard goat's cheese
2 tbsp pumpkin seeds
1 medium-hot chilli, finely chopped
1 tbsp olive oil
1 garlic clove, crushed
2 tsp chopped flat-leaf parsley
coarse sea salt and black pepper

The roasted peppers come from Tamar Shany, a multitalented chef who is equally at ease in both the pastry and the savoury sections. She is the one who set up our Kensington kitchen, her 'baby'.

Both the peppers and the cannellini bean paste are excellent fridge staples that keep well, so you can make this up quickly as a last-minute starter. The quantities below will give you enough bean spread for the bruschettas plus extra for the fridge.

Roasted pepper and cannellini bruschetta

serves 4

1   Drain the beans and place in a large saucepan with enough cold water to cover them by twice their volume. Bring to the boil and simmer for 80–90 minutes, until they are very soft. You will need to skim the froth from the surface a few times during the cooking and might have to add some more boiling water. Drain the beans but keep the cooking liquid.

2   Heat the oven to 200°C/Gas Mark 6. To prepare the peppers, cut them into quarters and shave off the white parts and the seeds. Put them in a roasting tray and toss with 2 tablespoons of the oil and a little salt. Roast in the oven for 35 minutes or until soft, then transfer the hot peppers to a bowl and cover it with cling film; this will make them easier to peel. Once they are cool enough to handle, peel the peppers, place in a container with their cooking juices and set aside. In a separate bowl whisk 60ml of the olive oil with the balsamic vinegar, water, sugar, thyme, 2 sliced garlic cloves and a pinch of salt. Pour this marinade over the peppers and leave for at least half an hour. If you are not using them on the day, keep the peppers refrigerated for up to a week, making sure they are well immersed in the marinade.

3   Put the warm beans in a food processor together with 1 crushed garlic clove, the lemon juice, the remaining oil, 1 teaspoon of salt, a good grinding of black pepper and 50ml of the bean cooking liquid. Process to a smooth paste. Taste and see if you want to add any more salt, pepper or lemon juice. Leave to cool and then taste again; you will probably need to add more salt.

4   Put the bread slices on a baking tray, brush them with olive oil and sprinkle with a little salt. Bake for 10–12 minutes or until golden brown. While they are still hot, rub the slices with 2 peeled garlic cloves, then leave them to cool on a wire rack.

5   Spread a good amount of the bean purée on each toast, top generously with the marinated peppers, then garnish with the spring onions and a drizzle of olive oil.

150g dried cannellini beans, soaked overnight in plenty of cold water
2 red and 2 yellow peppers
135ml olive oil, plus extra for brushing
2 tbsp balsamic vinegar
2 tbsp water
1 tsp muscovado sugar
4 sprigs of thyme
5 garlic cloves
juice of 1 lemon
4 thick slices of Crusty white Italian loaf ↗ page 162 or another rustic loaf
2 spring onions, roughly sliced
salt and pepper

Deliciously rich, this can be made even richer by using mascarpone instead of the cream cheese. Serve as a light, summery main course or cut smaller pieces of bread for party finger food.

Organic salmon and asparagus bruschetta

serves 4

1 Preheat the oven to 200°C/Gas Mark 6. Drizzle an ovenproof dish with some olive oil and place the salmon fillet in it, skin-side down. Add the bay leaves, juniper and wine, then sprinkle the fillet with a little salt. Squeeze over the lemon half and throw it in with the fish. Cover the dish with foil and bake for 15–20 minutes. The fish should be just cooked, and still lightly pink inside. Remove from the oven, take off the foil and allow to cool.
2 To prepare the bread, lay out the slices on a baking tray, brush with olive oil and sprinkle with salt. Bake for 10–12 minutes, until golden brown. While they are still hot, rub the slices with the peeled garlic cloves, then leave on a wire rack to cool down.
3 Trim off the woody ends of the asparagus. Add the asparagus to a large saucepan of boiling salted water and simmer for 2 minutes. Drain in a colander and refresh under cold water until completely cool. Drain again and leave to dry in a colander.
4 When the salmon has cooled sufficiently, flake it with your hands into big chunks, reserving the cooking liquor in a separate bowl.
5 Spread the toasts liberally with the cream cheese. Arrange the salmon and asparagus on top creatively. Spoon over some of the reserved cooking juices and finish with a good grind of black pepper and some salt. Garnish with a few sprigs of chervil and a wedge of lemon.

olive oil for drizzling and brushing the bread
350g organic salmon fillet
4 bay leaves
4 juniper berries
120ml Muscat or another sweet wine
½ lemon
4 thick slices of Crusty white Italian loaf ↗ page 162 **or another rustic loaf**
2 garlic cloves, peeled
150g asparagus spears
120g cream cheese
coarse sea salt and black pepper
a few sprigs of chervil and lemon wedges, to garnish

Olive oil crackers, Parmesan and poppy biscuits (↗ overleaf)

Chapter 3   Baking and patisserie

In our first year in Notting Hill, we used to cut these savoury biscuits into odd-shaped, long strips, then bake and pile them up inside a large black African bowl and place in the window. It looked spectacular. Only one problem: they were so delicate they broke within an hour. So here we roll them into a more practical, though still beautifully elegant, shape. They are so easy to make you'll never need to buy crackers again. They are perfect fresh from the oven, as crisp as can be, served with cheese or dips.

Olive oil crackers

makes about 25

1 In a large bowl, mix together all the ingredients except the sea salt to form a soft dough. You can do this by hand or in a mixer fitted with a dough hook. Work it until you get a firm consistency, then cover with cling film and leave to rest in the fridge for 1 hour.
2 Heat up the oven to 220°C/Gas Mark 7. Turn the dough on to a clean work surface. Have a bowl of flour for dusting ready at the side. Use a large, sharp knife to cut off walnut-sized pieces (roughly 15g each) from the dough. Roll out each piece as thinly as possible with a rolling pin, dusting with plenty of flour. They should end up looking like long, oval tongues, almost paper thin.
3 Place the crackers on a tray lined with baking parchment. Brush them with plenty of olive oil and sprinkle with sea salt. Bake for about 6 minutes, until crisp and golden.

250g plain flour, plus extra for dusting
1 tsp baking powder
115ml water
25ml olive oil, plus extra for brushing
½ tsp salt
1 tsp paprika
¼ tsp cayenne pepper
¼ tsp black pepper
coarse sea salt for sprinkling

These are to have with drinks and they are more addictive than
a fine Bordeaux. Beware! For the freshest of biscuits, always keep
a log of the dough in the freezer ready to defrost and bake.

The poppy seeds are not essential but they do make the biscuits
a bit more celebratory.

Parmesan and poppy biscuits

makes about 35

1 Sift the flour, baking powder, paprika and cayenne into a bowl and
   add the salt and pepper.
2 Mix the softened butter with the Parmesan until they are well blended.
   You can do this either by hand, using a spatula, or in a freestanding
   mixer fitted with the paddle attachment. Add the dry ingredients and
   continue mixing until a soft dough is formed.
3 Put the dough on a well-floured work surface and divide it in half. Use
   plenty of flour, both on your hands and on the work surface, to roll
   each piece into a long log, 3–4cm in diameter. Wrap each log in cling
   film and place in the fridge for about 30 minutes to firm up.
4 Scatter the poppy seeds over a flat plate or tray. Brush the logs with
   the beaten egg and then roll them in the poppy seeds until covered.
   Refrigerate again for 1 hour (at this stage you can also wrap the logs
   and freeze them).
5 Preheat the oven to 170°C/Gas Mark 3. Line a baking sheet with
   baking parchment. Cut the logs into slices 5–8mm thick and arrange
   them on the tray, spaced 3cm apart. Bake for 12 minutes. The biscuits
   should be dark golden and smell amazing! Leave to cool completely
   before serving, or storing in a tightly sealed container.

**210g plain flour, plus plenty
   extra for dusting**
½ tsp baking powder
½ tsp paprika
a pinch of cayenne pepper
a pinch of salt
**½ tsp freshly ground
   black pepper**
**165g unsalted butter, at room
   temperature**
**165g Parmesan cheese,
   freshly grated**
80g poppy seeds
1 free-range egg, beaten

Utterly tasty, especially when just out of the oven. While they're baking, your kitchen will be filled with mouthwatering aromas. If the straws aren't devoured at once, heat them up slightly just before serving.

Claudine, who tried the recipe while in France so couldn't get Cheddar, used mature Comté instead and said they were delectable.

One little piece of advice: when making the cheese straws, work fast and try to keep a flow of fresh, cool air in the kitchen. Otherwise the pastry will heat up and turn sticky and difficult to manage.

Cheddar and caraway cheese straws

makes 10

plain flour for dusting
300g puff pastry, or ½ quantity of Rough puff pastry ↗ page 280
1 free-range egg, lightly beaten
100g strong Cheddar cheese, finely grated
1 tsp caraway seeds

1 Dust a work surface lightly with flour and roll out the pastry to a rectangle 2–3mm thick. Trim the edges with a sharp knife in order to get a perfect rectangle, roughly 30 × 20cm. Place on a baking sheet dusted with flour and leave to rest in the fridge for 30 minutes.

2 Return the pastry sheet to the dusted work surface. Brush off any flour and then brush the top with the beaten egg and sprinkle over half the cheese. Press the cheese down lightly with your hands so it sticks to the pastry. Be brisk so that you don't warm up the butter in the pastry. Carefully turn the pastry over, brush off any excess flour and repeat this process on the other side.

3 Now cut strips about 3cm wide across the width of the pastry. Pick up a strip holding one end in each hand. Place one end on the work surface and hold still. Twist the other end on the work surface to make a tight spiral form. You will need to pull as you twist to get a long, hollow, straw shape.

4 Carefully transfer the straws to a baking sheet lined with baking parchment. Space them at least 3cm apart and sprinkle with the caraway seeds. Rest them in the fridge for at least 30 minutes.

5 Preheat the oven to 180°C/Gas Mark 4. Place the tray of cheese straws in the oven and bake for 20–25 minutes. Make sure you do not open the oven door for the first 15 minutes. When ready, the straws should be a beautiful light brown colour. Let them cool slightly before serving.

Chapter 3   Baking and patisserie

The olive oil gives this cake extra depth and intensity. The complex flavours mature over time, so consider wrapping the cake in cling film and refrigerating it, ready to ice and serve, for up to three days. Somewhat less festive (and less calorie laden), this is still very satisfying without the maple icing. Just dust lightly with icing sugar.

Apple and olive oil cake with maple icing

serves 6–8

1 Grease a 20cm springform cake tin and line the base and sides with baking parchment. Place the sultanas and water in a medium saucepan and simmer over a low heat until all of the water has been absorbed. Leave to cool.

2 Preheat the oven to 170°C/Gas Mark 3. Sift together the flour, cinnamon, salt, baking powder and bicarbonate of soda and set aside.

3 Put the oil and sugar in the bowl of a freestanding electric mixer fitted with a paddle attachment (or use a whisk if you don't have a mixer). Slit the vanilla pod lengthways in half and, using a sharp knife, scrape the seeds out into the bowl. Beat the oil, sugar and vanilla together, then gradually add the eggs. The mix should be smooth and thick at this stage. Mix in the diced apples, sultanas and lemon zest, then lightly fold in the sifted dry ingredients.

4 Whisk the egg whites in a clean bowl, either by hand or with a mixer, until they have a soft meringue consistency. Fold them into the batter in 2 additions, trying to lose as little air as possible.

5 Pour the batter into the lined tin, level it with a palette knife and place in the oven. Bake for 1½ hours, or until a skewer inserted in the centre comes out clean. Remove from the oven and leave to cool in the tin.

6 Once the cake is completely cold, you can assemble it. Remove from the tin and use a large serrated knife to cut it horizontally in half. You should end up with 2 similar discs. If the cake is very domed, you might need to shave a bit off the top half to level it.

7 To make the icing, beat together the butter, muscovado sugar and maple syrup until light and airy. You can do this by hand, or, preferably, in a mixer, using the paddle attachment. Add the cream cheese and beat until the icing is totally smooth.

8 Using a palette knife, spread a 1cm-thick layer of icing over the bottom half of the cake. Carefully place the top half on it. Spoon the rest of the icing on top and use the palette knife to create a wave-like or any other pattern. Dust it with icing sugar, if you like.

80g sultanas
4 tbsp water
280g plain flour
½ tsp ground cinnamon
¼ tsp salt
½ tsp baking powder
1¼ tsp bicarbonate of soda
120ml olive oil
160g caster sugar
½ vanilla pod
2 free-range eggs, lightly beaten
3 Bramley apples, peeled, cored and cut into 1cm dice
grated zest of 1 lemon
2 free-range egg whites
icing sugar for dusting (optional)

Maple icing
100g unsalted butter, at room temperature
100g light muscovado sugar
85ml maple syrup
220g cream cheese, at room temperature

A beautiful-looking and even better-tasting cake. Use blood oranges when in season (January to April) for a spectacular effect.

Quick polenta (the Polenta Valsugana variety is widely available in the UK) works better in cakes than standard polenta. Because it cooks more quickly, it doesn't leave a gritty texture.

One important warning: Alison Quinn, who dedicatedly tried many recipes for us, used a loose-based tin when she made this cake but forgot to line the corners and sides of the tin with paper. The result was a little disaster. The caramel and the juices from the oranges leaked all over her brand new oven … a nasty cleaning job!

Orange polenta cake

1   Lightly grease a 20cm round cake tin and line the base and sides with baking parchment. If using a loose-based tin, make sure the paper circle you cut for the base is large enough to go some way up the sides as well, to prevent leaking.

2   To make the caramel, have ready by the stove a small pastry brush and a cup of water. Put the sugar for the caramel topping in a heavy-based saucepan and add the water. Stir gently to wet the sugar through and then place on a low-medium heat. Slowly bring the sugar to the boil. While it bubbles away, brush the sides of the pan occasionally with a little of the water in the cup to get rid of any crystals that form close to the bubbling sugar. After a few minutes the water should evaporate and the sugar will start to darken. Be sure to keep your eyes on the sugar at all times as it can easily burn. As soon as it reaches a nice golden colour, remove the pan from the heat. With your face at a safe distance, add the chunks of butter. Stir with a wooden spoon and pour the caramel over the lined base of the cake tin. Carefully but quickly (so it doesn't set) tilt it to spread evenly.

3   Grate the zest of the 2 oranges, making sure you don't reach the white part of the skin. Set the grated zest aside. Using a small, sharp knife, slice off 1cm from the top and bottom of each orange. Standing each orange up on a board, carefully but neatly follow the natural curves of the orange with the knife to peel off the remaining skin and all the white pith. Cut each orange horizontally into roughly 6 slices. Remove the pips and lay out the slices tightly over the caramel. (You might need to peel and slice another orange to cover the whole space.)

4   Now move on to the cake batter. Heat up the oven to 170°C/Gas Mark 3. Sift together the flour, baking powder and salt and set aside.

5   In an electric mixer fitted with the paddle attachment, cream the butter and sugar together lightly. Make sure they are well combined but do not incorporate much air into the mixture. Gradually add the eggs while the machine is on a low speed. Next add the reserved orange zest and the orange blossom water, followed by the almonds, polenta and sifted dry ingredients. As soon as they are all mixed in, stop the machine.

6   Transfer the batter to the prepared cake tin, making sure that the oranges underneath stay in a single neat layer. Level the mixture carefully with a palette knife. Place the cake in the oven and bake for 40–45 minutes, until a skewer inserted in the centre comes out dry. Remove from the oven and leave to cool for about 5 minutes.

7   While the cake is still hot (warm it up a little if you forgot, otherwise the caramel will stick to the paper), place a cardboard disc or a flat plate on top. Briskly turn over and then remove the tin and the lining paper. Leave the cake to cool completely.

8   For the glaze, bring the marmalade and water to the boil in a small saucepan and then pass through a sieve. While the glaze is still hot, lightly brush the top of the cake with it.

serves 6–8

50g plain flour
1 tsp baking powder
½ tsp salt
200g unsalted butter
200g caster sugar
3 free-range eggs, lightly beaten
2 tsp orange blossom water
240g ground almonds
120g quick-cook polenta

Caramel topping
90g caster sugar
2 tbsp water
20g unsalted butter, diced
2 oranges, plus a possible extra one

Glaze (optional)
4 tbsp orange marmalade
1 tbsp water

This is a simple cake to prepare, and a most delectable one, made a bit more complicated by baking in two stages. The result is two chocolate layers with slightly different consistencies: one a bit firmer and cakey, the other more moussy. Chocolate connoisseurs will appreciate that. For a less discerning audience, or if you want to hasten the process or are feeling lazy, cook the whole cake at once. The result will still be highly satisfying.

Chocolate fudge cake

serves 6–8

1 Preheat the oven to 170°C/Gas Mark 3. Grease a 20cm springform cake tin and line the base and sides with baking parchment.
2 Place the butter and both types of chocolate in a very large heatproof bowl – it should be big enough to accommodate the entire mix. Put the brown sugar and water in a small saucepan, stir to mix, then bring to the boil over a medium heat. Pour the boiling syrup over the butter and chocolate and stir well until they have melted and you are left with a runny chocolate sauce. Stir in the egg yolks, one at a time. Set aside until the mixture comes to room temperature.
3 Put the egg whites and salt in a large bowl and whisk to a firm, but not too dry meringue. Using a rubber spatula or a large metal spoon, gently fold the meringue into the cooled chocolate mixture a third at a time. The whites should be fully incorporated but there is no harm if you can see small bits of meringue in the mix.
4 Pour 800g (about two-thirds) of the mixture into the prepared cake tin and level gently with a palette knife. Leave the rest of the batter for later. Place the cake in the oven and bake for about 40 minutes, until a skewer inserted in the centre comes out almost clean. Remove from the oven and leave to cool completely.
5 Flatten the top of the cake with a palette knife. Don't worry about breaking the crust. Pour the rest of the batter on top and level the surface again. Return to the oven and bake for 20–25 minutes. The cake should still have moist crumbs when checked with a skewer. Leave to cool completely before removing from the tin. Dust with cocoa powder and serve.
6 The cake will keep, covered, at room temperature for 4 days.

240g unsalted butter,
cut into small cubes
265g dark chocolate
(52 per cent cocoa solids),
cut into small pieces
95g dark chocolate
(70 per cent cocoa solids),
cut into small pieces
290g light muscovado sugar
4 tbsp water
5 large free-range eggs, separated
a pinch of salt
cocoa powder for dusting

Once you've baked this cake you'll be able to take your 'A' levels on the subject of caramel. You make it twice here, using different methods, but don't be scared. It is one of those things that seem intimidating from a distance but are actually not that hard to do. Just follow the instructions confidently yet cautiously. A note of advice: to get the caramel off your pans, fill them up with water and boil on the stove. Remove the water and wash normally.

Felicity Gray, who tried this cake for us, said it was scrummy. We couldn't agree more.

Caramel and macadamia cheesecake

serves 8

600g good-quality cream cheese, at room temperature
120g caster sugar
½ vanilla pod
4 free-range eggs, lightly beaten
60ml soured cream
icing sugar for dusting

Base
160g dry biscuits (HobNobs are good)
40g unsalted butter, melted

Nut topping
150g macadamia nuts
90g caster sugar

Caramel sauce
65g unsalted butter
160g caster sugar
100ml whipping cream

1 Preheat the oven to 140°C/Gas Mark 1. Lightly grease a 20cm springform cake tin and line the base and sides with baking parchment.
2 To make the base, whiz the biscuits to crumbs in a food processor (or put them in a plastic bag and bash with a mallet or rolling pin). Mix with the melted butter to a wet, sandy consistency. Transfer to the lined tin and flatten with the back of a tablespoon to create a level base.
3 To make the cake batter, put the sugar and cream cheese in a mixing bowl. Slit the vanilla pod lengthways in half and, using a sharp knife, scrape the seeds out into the bowl. Whisk by hand or, more easily, with an electric mixer, until smooth. Gradually add the eggs and soured cream, whisking until smooth. Pour the mixture over the biscuit base and place in the oven. Bake for 60–70 minutes, until set; a skewer inserted in the centre should come out with a slightly wet crumb attached. Leave to cool to room temperature, then turn out of the tin. Removing the cake from its base can be a little tricky. You can leave it there and serve from the base, if you prefer. Otherwise, get a flat 20cm cake board and gently squeeze it between the base of the cake and the lining paper. As a last resort, get a couple of fish slices and someone to help you lift the whole thing on to a flat serving plate. Now chill the cake for at least a couple of hours.
4 To prepare the nut topping, scatter the nuts over a baking sheet and roast in the oven at 140°C/Gas Mark 1 for about 15 minutes, until golden. Remove from the oven and set aside. Line a baking tray with baking parchment. Place the sugar in a saucepan with a very thick base (it is important that the layer of sugar is not more than 3mm high in the pan, so choose a large one). Heat the sugar gently until it turns into a golden-brown caramel. Do not stir it at any stage. Don't worry if some small bits of sugar don't totally dissolve. Carefully add the toasted nuts and mix gently with a wooden spoon. When most of the nuts are coated in caramel, pour them on to the lined tray and leave to set. Break bits off and chop them very roughly with a large knife. It's nice to leave some of the nuts just halved or even whole.
5 To make the sauce, put the butter and sugar in a thick-bottomed saucepan and stir constantly over a medium heat with a wooden spoon until it becomes a smooth, dark caramel. The butter and sugar will look as if they have split. Don't worry; just keep on stirring. Once the desired colour is reached, carefully add the cream while stirring vigorously. Remove from the heat and leave to cool.
6 To finish the cake, dust the edges and sides with plenty of icing sugar. Spoon the sauce in the centre, allowing it to spill over a little. Scatter lots of caramelised nuts on top. The cheesecake will keep in the fridge for 3 days.

There are two warring camps at Ottolenghi over the vital issue of …
carrot cake. Helen Goh and Sarit Packer, who are always on the lookout
for new ideas and some earth-shattering recipes, like their carrot cakes
dense and fruity. We prefer them light and fluffy, like this one. So far the
issue hasn't been resolved – there's just a tense ceasefire. Watch out for
the next Ottolenghi cookbook: if the balance of power shifts, you might
find a totally different carrot cake.

Carrot and walnut cake

serves 6–8

1 Preheat the oven to 170°C/Gas Mark 3. Grease a 20cm springform
   cake tin and line the base and sides with baking parchment.
2 Sift together the flour, baking powder, bicarbonate of soda and spices.
   Lightly whisk the whole egg with the egg yolk.
3 Put the sunflower oil and caster sugar in the bowl of an electric
   mixer fitted with the beater attachment and beat for about a minute
   on a medium speed. On a low speed, slowly add the beaten egg.
   Mix in the walnuts, coconut and carrot and then the sifted dry
   ingredients. Don't over mix.
4 Transfer the mixture to a large bowl. Wash and dry the mixer bowl,
   making sure it is totally clean, then put the egg whites and salt in
   it and whisk on a high speed until firm peaks form. Gently fold the
   egg whites into the carrot mixture in 3 additions, being careful not
   to over mix. Streaks of white in the mixture are okay.
5 Pour the cake mixture into the prepared tin and bake for approximately
   1 hour; it could take longer. A skewer inserted in the centre should
   come out dry. If the cake starts getting dark before the centre is
   cooked through, cover it with foil. Let the cake cool completely and
   then remove from the tin.
6 To make the icing, beat the cream cheese in a mixer until light and
   smooth. Remove from the mixer. Beat the butter, icing sugar and
   honey in the mixer until light and airy. Fold together the cheese and
   butter mixes. Spread waves of icing on top of the cake and sprinkle
   with the nuts.

160g plain flour
½ tsp baking powder
½ tsp bicarbonate of soda
1 tsp ground cinnamon
¼ tsp ground cloves
1 large free-range egg
1 free-range egg yolk
200g sunflower oil
270g caster sugar
50g walnuts, chopped
50g desiccated coconut
135g carrot, roughly grated
2 free-range egg whites
a pinch of salt

Icing
175g cream cheese,
   at room temperature
70g unsalted butter
35g icing sugar
25g honey
30g walnuts, chopped
   and lightly toasted

Teacakes

We are not sure how we came to call these teacakes – they are definitely not related to the British fruited bun bearing the name. In any case, these distinctively shaped individual cakes have become one of Ottolenghi's trademarks and are now made by many other patisseries. In America, the bundt tins that we use for making these cakes come in many different sizes, from giant family size to tiny petits fours. Ours are medium-small, taking 150–200g of cake batter, enough for one generous serving.

Bundt tins are not so easy to find in the UK but a very close alternative you can use for making them is a 10cm-diameter mini kugelhopf pan, made by Baker's Pride. It is available online at www.uktvcookshop.co.uk and other sites. We sometimes get them from Bob at Kitchen Ideas on Westbourne Grove, who is always fantastically helpful and has a huge selection of domestic and professional kitchen equipment.

The bundt or kugelhopf's volcano-like shape allows you to play creatively with different icings and glazes. Still, you could do the same with other tins or moulds of similar capacity. These cakes can even be made like muffins in paper cases, in which case you would probably get more than six.

It is important to grease bundt tins well before filling them. We chill the tins first and then brush them generously with melted butter.

Peach and raspberry

makes 6

1 Preheat the oven to 170°C/Gas Mark 3. Leave 6 small bundt or kugelhopf tins in the fridge for a few minutes, then remove and brush with plenty of melted butter. Return them to the fridge.

2 Start by sifting together the flour, baking powder, bicarbonate of soda and salt, then set aside. Cream the butter and sugar together until light and fluffy, preferably using an electric mixer. Mix the eggs with the vanilla, then gradually add to the creamed mixture, beating well until each little addition has been fully incorporated. Gently fold in a third of the flour mixture, followed by a third of the soured cream. Continue like this until both are mixed in and the batter is smooth. Fold in the diced peach.

3 Either pipe or spoon the mixture into the tins, filling them to about 2cm from the top. Press 4 raspberries into each cake, sinking them with your finger to just below the surface of the batter (keep the remaining raspberries to scatter over the finished cakes). Place the cakes in the oven and bake for 25–30 minutes. Poke with a skewer to make sure they are completely dry inside; it should come out clean. Remove them from the oven and leave in their tins for 10 minutes to cool slightly, then turn out on to a wire rack and leave to cool completely.

4 To make the glaze, place all the ingredients in a small saucepan and bring to the boil. Stir and leave to simmer for 4 minutes. Pass the hot glaze through a fine sieve, rubbing the raspberry pips with a wooden spoon to release as much of the juice as you can. Brush or drizzle the hot glaze over the cakes and leave to set (if the glaze is too thin to coat the cakes, simmer it over a moderate heat until reduced; if it is too thick, add a little water and heat gently). Pile the remaining raspberries on top of the cakes and dust with icing sugar.

180g unsalted butter,
  plus melted butter
  for greasing the tins
260g plain flour
1 tsp baking powder
½ tsp bicarbonate of soda
¼ tsp salt
160g caster sugar
2 free-range eggs
1 tsp vanilla essence
170ml soured cream
1 peach, halved, stoned
  and cut into 1cm dice
250g raspberries
icing sugar for dusting

Glaze
200g raspberries
170g apricot jam
100ml water

Lemon and blueberry

makes 6

1 Preheat the oven to 170°C/Gas Mark 3. Leave 6 small bundt or kugelhopf tins in the fridge for a few minutes, then remove and brush with plenty of melted butter. Return them to the fridge.

2 Mix together the flour and ground almonds and set aside. Using an electric mixer, or by hand, cream the butter and sugar together until pale and fluffy. Break the eggs into a cup and mix lightly with a fork. Gradually add the eggs to the butter mix, beating well until each little addition has been fully incorporated. If the mixture looks as if it has split, add a little of the almond and flour mixture and it should come back together. Once all the egg is incorporated, gently fold in the almonds and flour, followed by the lemon zest, juice and blueberries. Be gentle, so the blueberries don't break.

3 Take the moulds from the fridge. Either pipe or spoon the mixture into the tins, reaching all the way up to the edge. Level the mixture and clean the edges of the tins if necessary. Bake in the oven for 30–35 minutes, until a skewer inserted into the centre of a cake comes out clean. Remove them from the oven and leave them in their tins for 10 minutes, then turn out on to a wire rack and leave to cool completely.

4 To make the glaze, whisk the lemon juice and icing sugar together in a small bowl, adding more lemon juice or sugar if necessary to make an icing with a drizzling consistency. Spoon it liberally over the cakes or brush with a pastry brush, letting the icing drip down the sides.

280g unsalted butter, plus melted butter for greasing the tins
65g plain flour
280g ground almonds
280g caster sugar
5 free-range eggs
grated zest of 2 lemons
100ml lemon juice
120g blueberries

Glaze
50ml lemon juice
150g icing sugar

Lavender and honey

makes 6

1 Preheat the oven to 170°C/Gas Mark 3. Leave 6 small bundt or kugelhopf tins in the fridge for a few minutes, then remove and brush with plenty of melted butter. Return them to the fridge.

2 Cream the butter, sugar and honey together until pale and fluffy, preferably using an electric mixer. Break the eggs into a cup, beat them lightly with a fork and gradually add to the creamed mixture, beating well until each little addition has been fully incorporated. Sift together the flour, baking powder, bicarbonate of soda, salt and cinnamon, then stir in the dried lavender. Gently fold the flour mixture into the creamed mix in 3 additions, alternating with the soured cream.

3 Either pipe or spoon the mixture into the tins, filling them to about 1.5cm from the top. Level out the mix and clean the edges of the tins if necessary. Place in the oven and bake for 25–30 minutes, until a skewer inserted in the centre of a cake comes out clean. Remove them from the oven and leave in their tins for 10 minutes, then turn out on to a wire rack and leave to cool completely.

4 To make the glaze, mix the lemon juice and honey together in a small bowl, then whisk in enough icing sugar to make a thick, pourable glaze. Use a pastry brush or a spoon to coat the top of the cakes, allowing the icing to drip down the sides. Sprinkle with a little dried lavender.

225g unsalted butter, plus melted butter for greasing the tins
115g caster sugar
115g lavender honey (or plain honey if you can't get it)
3 free-range eggs
245g plain flour
1 tsp baking powder
½ tsp bicarbonate of soda
½ tsp salt
½ tsp ground cinnamon
½ tsp chopped dried lavender, plus extra to finish
110ml soured cream

Glaze
20ml lemon juice
2 tsp honey
about 100g icing sugar

Muffins

What makes muffins so attractive to home bakers is that they are quick, dead easy to make, require very little preparation and can be done with the most basic kitchen equipment (no need for a mixer or blender).

Unlike other cakes, it's best not to incorporate much air into a muffin batter, or to work the flour and develop the protein in it. For this reason, it is essential that at the last stage, when mixing the dry and wet ingredients together, you keep the stirring to a minimum. The key is to stop while there are still plenty of unmixed lumps. This will give the muffins their typical light and short texture.

The plum muffin below has a celebration look. To turn it into a casual breakfast, skip the compote topping and serve plain (and still delicious).

Use dark red, ripe plums for the best visual effect. As for the marzipan, try to avoid the luminous yellow stuff, artificial in substance and flavour. Crazy Jack organic marzipan tastes good and is available from health-food shops and some supermarkets.

Plum, marzipan and cinnamon

makes 10–12

1 Make the plum compote first. Preheat the oven to 170°C/Gas Mark 3. Place the plums in a shallow baking dish, add the sugar and cinnamon stick and mix together. Place in the oven and bake for 10–20 minutes, until the plums are soft and their skin starts to separate from the flesh (the cooking time will vary significantly, depending on the ripeness of the fruit). Remove from the oven and set aside to cool.
2 Sift the flour, baking powder, bicarbonate of soda, cinnamon and salt into a bowl. Put the sugar and eggs in a large mixing bowl and whisk together. Add the milk and butter (make sure it is not too hot) and whisk to combine.
3 Grate the marzipan on the coarse side of a grater and add this to the batter, together with the orange zest. Now add 80g of the plum compote (pulp and juices) and stir together. Set the rest of the compote aside for later.
4 Using a rubber spatula, gently fold the flour mixture into the wet mix until just combined (there may still be a few lumps and bits of flour; that is what you want).
5 Line your muffin tins with paper cases and spoon in the mixture, filling them all the way to the top. Bake for 25–30 minutes, until a skewer inserted in the centre of a muffin comes out clean. When cool enough to handle, take the muffins out of the tins and leave on a wire rack until cold.
6 Just before serving, dust the tops with a little icing sugar and top with the reserved cooked plums.

480g plain flour
1 tsp baking powder
½ tsp bicarbonate of soda
1 tsp ground cinnamon
a pinch of salt
200g caster sugar
2 free-range eggs
110g unsalted butter, melted
280ml milk
grated zest of 2 oranges
120g marzipan
icing sugar for dusting

Plum compote
700g ripe red plums, stoned and cut into quarters
60g caster sugar
1 cinnamon stick

Blueberries are the all-time favourite muffin flavour. The reason is their unique ability to keep their shape and most of their wonderful characteristics through the baking process.

Blueberry crumble

makes 10–12

1 Preheat the oven to 170°C/Gas Mark 3. Line a muffin tray with paper cases.
2 Sift together the flour, baking powder and salt and set aside. In a large mixing bowl, lightly whisk together the eggs, sugar and melted butter (make sure it is not too hot). Whisk in the milk and lemon zest, then gently fold in the fruit.
3 Add the sifted dry ingredients and fold together very gently. Make sure you stir the mix just enough to combine; it should remain lumpy and rough.
4 Spoon the mixture into the muffin cases to fill them up. Generously cover with the crumble topping to form small domes over the batter, then dot with a few extra blueberries. Bake for 30–35 minutes or until a skewer inserted in the centre of a muffin comes out clean. Take out of the tins while still warm.

540g plain flour
5 tsp baking powder
½ tsp salt
2 free-range eggs
340g caster sugar
140g unsalted butter, melted
380ml milk
grated zest of 1 lemon
1 Granny Smith apple (unpeeled),
  cut into 1cm dice
200g fresh blueberries, plus
  a few extra for the topping
½ quantity of Crumble ↗ page 279

A wholesome option but extremely tasty, with lots of spice and tons of flavour. Beware, you will end up eating much more than you intended to. Thanks to Tamar Shany, for developing this recipe during one of her sleepless nights in Notting Hill.

Carrot, apple and pecan

makes 10–12

1 Start by making the topping. In a bowl, stir together the butter, flour and sugar. Rub with your fingertips until the butter is incorporated and you have a crumbly texture. Mix in the oats and seeds and then the water, oil and honey. Stir everything together, resulting in a wet, sandy texture. Set aside.

2 Preheat the oven to 170°C/Gas Mark 3. Line a muffin tray with paper cases.

3 Sift together the flour, baking powder, cinnamon and salt. In a large mixing bowl, whisk together the eggs, oil, sugar, vanilla and grated carrot and apple. Gently fold in the pecans, sultanas, coconut and then the sifted flour mixture. Do not over mix, and don't worry if the batter is lumpy and irregular. Spoon into the lined tins and scatter the topping generously over the top. Bake for about 25 minutes, until a skewer inserted in the centre of a muffin comes out clean. Remove the muffins from the tins when they are just warm and allow them to cool down before serving. Their flavour will actually improve after a couple of hours.

300g plain flour
2 tsp baking powder
2 tsp ground cinnamon
a pinch of salt
4 free-range eggs
160ml sunflower oil
280g caster sugar
2 tsp vanilla essence
220g peeled carrot, grated
200g Bramley or Granny Smith
  apples, roughly grated
100g pecan nuts,
  roughly chopped
100g sultanas
50g flaked coconut

Topping
50g unsalted butter, cut into
  small pieces
75g plain flour
25g light muscavado sugar
50g whole rolled oats
15g sunflower seeds
25g pumpkin seeds
15g black sesame seeds
1 tsp water
1 tsp sunflower oil
1½ tbsp honey

Cupcakes

The secret of a good cupcake is in the icing. Ours are a bit serious, with no food colouring and frilly decorations but still madly rich and creamy and luscious. We also love the over-the-top American cupcakes, like the ones at the Magnolia Bakery in New York or the Hummingbird Bakery on Portobello Road in London. Whichever version you choose, don't torment yourself, you only live once!

Hazelnut

makes 8–12

1 Preheat the oven to 150°C/Gas Mark 2. Place the hazelnuts on a baking sheet and roast for 15 minutes, until lightly coloured. Remove from the oven. Once they have thoroughly cooled down, rub them in a tea towel and shake it in your hands to get rid of most of the skins. Blitz them in a food processor with half the sugar until finely chopped.

2 Now make the cupcakes. Increase the oven temperature to 170°C/ Gas Mark 3. Line a muffin tray or bun sheet with 8–12 paper cases. Sift together the flour, baking powder and salt. Cream together the butter, remaining sugar, hazelnut oil and finely chopped hazelnuts until light and airy. Mix in the beaten eggs a little at a time, waiting until each addition is fully incorporated before adding the next bit. Use a spatula or large metal spoon to fold in half the sifted dry ingredients, then half the soured cream, followed by the rest of the dry ingredients and then the remaining cream. Spoon the mixture into the cupcake cases, filling them to within 5mm of the rim. Bake for 20–25 minutes, until a skewer inserted in the centre comes out clean. Remove from the oven and leave to cool.

3 Make the icing only once the cupcakes are cold. Beat the cream cheese and mascarpone together until they are smooth and light. In a separate bowl, beat the butter and icing sugar together, either with an electric mixer or by hand, for at least 5 minutes (if the whisk doesn't reach the bottom of the bowl you might need to do this by hand). The mixture should turn almost white and become fluffy and light. Fold in the cream cheese mixture and then use a spatula to sculpt a wavy topping on each cupcake.

45g unblanched hazelnuts
150g caster sugar
180g plain flour
1 ¼ tsp baking powder
⅓ tsp salt
150g unsalted butter
1 tbsp hazelnut oil
2 small free-range eggs,
  lightly beaten
150ml soured cream

Icing
150g cream cheese, at room
  temperature
150g mascarpone cheese,
  at room temperature
80g unsalted butter, at room
  temperature
100g icing sugar

Chocolate

1 Heat the oven to 170°C/Gas Mark 3. Line a muffin tray or a bun sheet with 12 paper cases.

2 Whisk together the first 7 ingredients in a large mixing bowl until they are just combined. Don't over mix. Sift together the flour, cocoa, baking powder and bicarbonate of soda. Add them to the wet mix, along with the salt and almonds, and fold together gently. Fold in the chocolate pieces.

3 Spoon the batter into the cupcake cases, filling them up completely. Bake for about 20–25 minutes; if you insert a skewer in one, it should come out with quite a bit of crumb attached. Remove from the oven and leave to cool, then take the cupcakes out of their tins.

4 While the cupcakes are in the oven, start making the icing. It will take time to set and become spreadable. Place the chocolate in a heatproof bowl. Put the cream in a small saucepan and heat almost to boiling point, then pour it over the chocolate. Use a rubber spatula to stir until all the chocolate has melted. Add the butter and Amaretto and beat until smooth.

5 Transfer the icing to a clean bowl and cover the surface with cling film. Leave at room temperature until the cupcakes have fully cooled down and the icing has started to set. You want to catch it at the point when it spreads easily but isn't hard. Do not rush it by refrigerating!

6 Spoon a generous amount of icing on top of each cupcake and shape with a palette knife.

2 free-range eggs
115ml soured cream
80ml sunflower oil
20ml black treacle
20g unsalted butter, melted
60g caster sugar
60g light muscovado sugar
120g plain flour
35g cocoa powder
1 tsp baking powder
½ tsp bicarbonate of soda
¼ tsp salt
40g ground almonds
**200g dark chocolate,
    cut into small pieces**

Icing
**165g dark chocolate,
    cut into small pieces**
135ml whipping cream
35g unsalted butter, diced
1 tbsp Amaretto liqueur

CHOCOLATE and
HAZELNUT BROWNIE
£2.10

For us, this is the cake God had in mind when inventing tea. It is the ideal counterpart for a late-in-the-day cup – pure warmth, comfort and reassurance. Or, worth considering too, serve warm with melting ice cream at the end of a good meal.

Instead of two small tins, you can also use one large one, in which case increase the baking time by 5–10 minutes.

Pear and Amaretto crumble cake

makes 2 small loaves (4–6 servings)

1 Preheat the oven to 170°C/Gas Mark 3. Grease 2 small (500g) loaf tins with melted butter and line the base and sides with baking parchment.
2 Mix the chopped apple and pear with the walnuts, lemon zest and Amaretto liqueur. In a separate bowl, sift together the flour, baking powder, cinnamon and cloves. Add the ground almonds.
3 Separate 2 of the eggs, keeping the whites separate while mixing the yolks with the third egg. Using an electric mixer, beat together the oil and sugar for about a minute (this can also be done by hand, mixing briskly with a spatula). On a low speed, slowly add the yolk and egg mix. Quickly add the sifted dry ingredients, followed by the fruit mix. Stop the machine as soon as everything is incorporated.
4 Whisk the egg whites with the salt until it forms firm peaks, then gently fold it into the cake mix, using a spatula or metal spoon. Again, be careful not to over mix. Streaks of white in the mixture are okay.
5 Divide the cake mix between the tins and scatter the crumble on top. Bake for 40–45 minutes, until a skewer inserted in the centre comes out clean (it might take a bit longer, depending on the moisture content of the fruit). If the cakes start going dark before the centre is cooked, cover them with foil. Remove from the oven and leave to cool, then remove the cakes from the tins.

melted butter for greasing the tins
100g (peeled weight) Bramley apple, peeled and cut into 1.5cm dice (about ½ apple)
150g (peeled weight) pear, peeled and cut into 1.5cm dice (about 1 pear)
30g toasted walnuts, roughly chopped
grated zest of 1 lemon
2 tbsp Amaretto liqueur
210g plain flour
¾ tsp baking powder
¾ tsp ground cinnamon
⅓ tsp ground cloves
45g ground almonds
3 free-range eggs
180ml sunflower oil
230g caster sugar
⅓ tsp salt
120g Crumble ↗ page 279

This is a rich cake – deliciously moist, with a depth of flavour formed by a mix of 'grown-up' ingredients such as Armagnac, prunes and treacle. But don't let this fool you; it is as moreish as any chocolate cake gets.

Agen prunes, from the southwest of France, are the best variety to use. They are juicy and tender and are widely available.

The recipe also works as one large loaf. You just need to bake the cake 5–10 minutes longer.

Sticky chocolate loaf

makes 2 small loaves (serves 4–6)

1 Preheat the oven to 170°C/Gas Mark 3. Butter 2 small (500g) loaf tins and line the base and sides with baking parchment.

2 Place half the prunes in a small saucepan and add the Armagnac or Cognac. Warm very slightly, then set aside.

3 Put the remaining prunes in a blender or food processor and blend together with the buttermilk or yoghurt and oil until you get a light, shiny paste, a bit like mayonnaise. Transfer to a large mixing bowl and, using a hand whisk, mix in the egg, both types of sugar and the treacle.

4 Sift together the flour, baking powder, bicarbonate of soda, salt and cocoa powder. Fold them gently into the prune mix with a spatula. Fold in the chopped chocolate and divide the mixture equally between the prepared tins. Level the surface with a spatula. Cut each soaked prune in half with scissors and use your fingers to press them below the surface of the cakes. Place in the oven and bake for 45–50 minutes, until a skewer inserted in the centre comes out clean.

5 While the cakes are in the oven, make the syrup. Mix the water and sugar in a small saucepan and place on the heat. As soon as the water begins to simmer and the sugar is completely dissolved, remove from the heat and set aside for 10 minutes to cool down slightly. Finally, stir in the Armagnac or Cognac (you can also add any liquid left from soaking the prunes).

6 As soon as the cakes are out of the oven, pierce them through in a few places with a skewer and use a pastry brush to soak them with the warm syrup. Let them cool down completely before removing from the tins.

220g Agen prunes, pitted
100ml Armagnac or Cognac
60ml buttermilk or yoghurt
60ml sunflower oil
1 free-range egg
30g caster sugar
60g light brown sugar
40ml treacle
115g plain flour
½ tsp baking powder
½ tsp bicarbonate of soda
a pinch of salt
15g cocoa powder
150g dark chocolate, chopped

Syrup
80ml water
80g caster sugar
2 tbsp Armagnac or Cognac

To make these biscuits, you shape the uncooked mixture into long logs and roll them in pistachios. Have a couple of those wrapped in cling film in the freezer, ready to thaw, slice and bake. There is nothing like a warm cookie!

Pistachio shortbreads

makes about 20

1 Use a pestle and mortar to crush the cardamom pods, then remove the skins and work the seeds to a fine powder.
2 Using an electric mixer with the beater attachment fitted, mix together the butter, ground rice, flour, salt, ground cardamom and icing sugar. Run the machine until they turn into a paste and then stop the mixer at once. You don't need to incorporate much air (you could also do this by hand using a large plastic scraper; a strong wrist is required!).
3 Turn out the dough and, dusting with a little flour, roll it with your hands into a log 3–4cm in diameter. Wrap in cling film and leave in the fridge for at least an hour.
4 While the dough is chilling, chop the pistachios finely with a sharp knife, but not as fine as ground almonds. Or, if using a food processor, pulse them a few times until ground with some chunkier bits remaining. Scatter the pistachios on a flat tray.
5 Brush the log with the beaten egg and roll it in the ground pistachios. Wrap back in cling film and leave in the fridge to set for at least 30 minutes.
6 Preheat the oven to 150°C/Gas Mark 2. Remove the cling film and cut the log into slices 5mm–1cm thick. Lay them out on a baking tray lined with baking parchment, spacing them at least 2cm apart. Dust with the vanilla sugar.
7 Bake the biscuits for roughly 20 minutes. They must not take on too much colour but should remain golden. Remove from the oven and allow to cool completely before storing in a sealed jar. They will keep for up to a week.

8 cardamom pods
200g unsalted butter
25g ground rice
240g plain flour
½ tsp salt
35g icing sugar
60g shelled pistachio nuts
1 free-range egg, lightly beaten
2 tbsp vanilla sugar

Pistachio and ginger biscotti (↗ page 224)

White chocolate and cranberry biscuits (↗ page 225)

This is not the traditional tooth-breaking Italian biscuit but a softer, friendlier version. Still, it counts as biscotti because it is baked twice: once as a log and then sliced into thin biscuits. Thank you to Helen for this marvellous recipe.

Pistachio and ginger biscotti

makes 25

1 Line a baking tray with baking parchment.
2 Using an electric mixer (or a good spatula and both your hands), cream the butter and sugar together until they lighten in colour and texture. Gradually add the eggs, beating well after each addition. Stir in the brandy and orange zest, followed by the flour, ground ginger and salt. Lastly, fold in the pistachios and stem ginger.
3 Lightly dust the lined baking tray with flour and spoon the mixture on to the tray. Leave to rest in the fridge for about 30 minutes so it firms up a little. Preheat the oven to 170°C/Gas Mark 3.
4 Take the dough out of the fridge and, using your hands and a bit of extra flour, form a log shape about 25cm long. It does not need to be perfect, as the mix will spread during baking. Bake for 20 minutes, then remove from the oven and leave to cool. At this point the log will be partially baked and still quite soft. Adjust the oven temperature to 130°C/Gas Mark ½.
5 Once the log has cooled down, use a serated knife to cut it across into slices 1cm thick. Lay them flat on the baking tray and return to the oven for about 40 minutes, until crisp. Remove and leave to cool. Store in a sealed container.

80g unsalted butter
110g caster sugar
2 free-range eggs, lightly beaten
1 tbsp brandy
grated zest of 1½ oranges
150g plain flour, plus extra for dusting
½ tsp ground ginger
¼ tsp salt
80g shelled pistachio nuts
60g stem ginger in syrup, drained and roughly chopped

This is a traditional recipe for chocolate chip cookies of the crunchy variety, only using white chocolate instead of dark, and adding dried cranberries for a little fruity freshness. The brown sugar gives them depth and a crisp texture. They are very popular with kids and adults alike. Have a container of shaped cookies in the freezer, ready to bake when you need them.

Dried blueberries make a good alternative to cranberries, making the biscuits more 'grown-up'.

White chocolate and cranberry biscuits

makes 25–30

1 Preheat the oven to 170°C/Gas Mark 3. Sift together the flour, salt, baking powder and bicarbonate of soda and set aside.
2 Put the butter, vanilla and sugars in a large mixing bowl and beat with a wooden spoon until the mixture is lighter in colour and texture. Gradually add the egg, making sure each addition is fully incorporated before adding more. Add the flour mixture and the oats, then the chocolate and cranberries. Do not continue mixing once the dry ingredients are blended in.
3 Chill the mixture slightly to help you shape the biscuits. Scoop out a bit of the mix with a spoon and use your hands to roll it into a ball, somewhere between the size of an olive and a walnut. Press the balls lightly on to baking trays lined with baking parchment. Make sure you space them a good 6–7cm apart (they will spread more than you expect!). Place in the oven and bake for about 10 minutes, until they are a good brown colour. Remove from the oven and allow to cool on the trays before serving.

90g plain flour
¼ tsp salt
½ tsp baking powder
½ tsp bicarbonate of soda
100g unsalted butter, at room temperature
1 tsp vanilla essence
110g soft brown sugar
25g caster sugar
1 egg, lightly beaten
80g whole rolled oats
60g white chocolate, chopped into chocolate-chip-sized pieces
75g dried cranberries

Chapter 3   Baking and patisserie

Not a traditional Florentine, this lace-like biscuit is the kind you just can't leave alone. Though its crisp lightness is quite extraordinary, you could brush one side with melted dark chocolate if you like, to justify the name and give it a more substantial texture.

They will keep for 4–5 days in an airtight container; just make sure you don't leave them out very long or they will lose their crispness.

Thanks to Jim for this recipe.

Almond and orange Florentines

makes about 20

vegetable oil for brushing
2 free-range egg whites
100g icing sugar
260g flaked almonds
grated zest of 1 orange

1 Preheat the oven to 150°C/Gas Mark 2. Line a heavy baking tray with baking parchment and brush lightly with vegetable oil. Next to you have a small bowl of cold water.

2 Put the egg whites, icing sugar, flaked almonds and orange zest in a bowl and gently mix them together. Dip your hand in the bowl of water and pick up portions of the mix to make little mounds on the lined tray, well spaced apart. Dip a fork in the water and flatten each biscuit very thinly. Try to make them as thin as possible without creating too many gaps between the almond flakes. They should be about 8cm in diameter.

3 Place the baking tray in the oven and bake for about 12 minutes, until the biscuits are golden brown. Check underneath one biscuit to make sure they are cooked through.

4 Allow to cool, then gently, using a palette knife, remove the biscuits from the baking sheet. Store in a sealed jar.

Choose the best dark chocolate you can find to make these marvellous truffles (well, not quite truffles, since they are squarish, but that's just a formality). We recommend one of Valrhona's Grand Cru or Amedei's Porcelana.

Champagne chocolates

makes about 40

60g milk chocolate
200g dark chocolate
150g unsalted butter
80ml champagne
40ml good-quality brandy

to finish
150g dark chocolate for coating
50g cocoa powder for dusting

1   Take a cake tin roughly 14cm square and line it with cling film. Using a sharp knife, chop both kinds of chocolate into small pieces and place them in a heatproof bowl large enough to accommodate all the ingredients. Warm the chocolate for a couple of minutes in a microwave or over a pan of simmering water until it is semi-melted; be careful not to heat it much. Cut the butter into small pieces and keep it separate.

2   Pour the champagne and brandy into a small saucepan and place on the stove until they warm up to around 80°C; they should be hot to the touch but not boiling. Pour the alcohol over the chocolate and stir gently with a rubber spatula until it melts completely. Stir in the butter in a few additions, then continue stirring until the mixture is smooth. Pour it into the lined tray and place in the fridge for at least 3 hours, until it has set firm.

3   Place the chocolate for coating in a mixing bowl and put it over a pan of simmering water. Stir occasionally and, as soon as the chocolate has melted, remove the bowl from the steam bath. Scatter the cocoa powder over a flat plate.

4   Turn the chilled chocolate block out of the tin on to a sheet of baking parchment and remove the cling film. Use a very sharp, long knife to cut it into roughly 2cm squares. Clean the knife in hot water after every time you cut.

5   Using 2 skewers or forks, dip the squares in the melted chocolate, wiping off any excess on the side of the bowl. Quickly roll the squares in the cocoa powder and place on a clean tray. Allow the chocolates to set in the fridge, but make sure you leave them out at room temperature for at least half an hour before serving.

Sour cherry amaretti (↗ page 232)

Chapter 3   Baking and patisserie

Prune and brandy truffles (↗ page 233)

This is our version of the popular little Italian biscuit. Serve them with coffee or, even better, break them over chocolate ice cream.

If you don't mind the effort, make your own ground almonds (blanch, peel and very lightly toast the almonds, then blitz them till they're fine). This will give a much deeper almond flavour. In any case, don't get carried away with the almond extract. Too much of it will give a terrible artificial aroma.

You can omit the sour cherries if you wish, or use dried apricots or dried blueberries instead.

Sour cherry amaretti

makes about 20

180g ground almonds
120g caster sugar
grated zest of 1 lemon
3 drops of natural almond extract
a pinch of salt
60g dried sour cherries,
   roughly chopped
2 free-range egg whites
2 tsp honey
plenty of icing sugar for rolling

1 Preheat the oven to 170°C/Gas Mark 3. Put the ground almonds, sugar, lemon zest, almond extract and salt in a large bowl and rub with your fingertips to disperse the zest and essence evenly. Add the cherries and set aside.

2 Using a manual or electric whisk, beat the egg whites and honey until they reach a soft meringue consistency. Gently fold the meringue into the almond mixture. At this stage you should have a soft, malleable paste.

3 With your hands, form the mixture into 20 irregular shapes. Roll them in plenty of icing sugar, then arrange them on a baking tray lined with baking parchment. Place in the oven and bake for about 12 minutes. The biscuits should have taken on some colour but remain relatively pale and chewy in the centre. Leave to cool completely before indulging, or storing them in a sealed jar.

We normally don't like mixing fruit and chocolate. There are exceptions, though. When the fruit isn't very acidic or juicy, it can easily carry the intensity of chocolate and its buttery texture. Agen prunes are perfect for this. The slow drying process gives them a mature, sweet aroma that lends itself dramatically well to the combination of chocolate and alcohol. Khalid Assyb invented this recipe for a special Christmas menu, a perfect time for this hefty indulgence.

Glucose syrup, available in many supermarkets, gives the chocolate ganache an extra-smooth texture. To get it out of the tub, wet your hand with water and lift a bit with your fingers. If you don't do this it will stick terribly.

Prune and brandy truffles

makes 24

24 Agen prunes
200g dark chocolate for coating
4 tbsp cocoa powder for dusting

Ganache filling
150g dark chocolate
20g unsalted butter
100ml double cream
4 tsp glucose syrup
4 tsp brandy

1 To make the ganache filling, chop up the chocolate and butter into very small pieces and place in a heatproof bowl. Put the cream and glucose into a small saucepan and bring to the boil, watching carefully. As soon as they boil, pour them over the chocolate and butter. Stir gently with a rubber spatula until you get a smooth, shiny mix (if the chocolate doesn't melt fully, you can 'help' it by placing the bowl over a saucepan of simmering water for a few seconds). Stir in the brandy until well blended. Place a sheet of cling film over the surface of the ganache and leave to set overnight at room temperature. Alternatively, you can set it in the fridge, but you will need to take it out in advance and let it come to room temperature before using.

2 Once the ganache has set, split each prune down one side with a knife and carefully remove the stone. Spoon some ganache into each prune to fill it up. Close to form a little parcel and then chill for at least half an hour.

3 To coat the prunes, roughly chop the dark chocolate and place in a bowl set over a saucepan of simmering water, making sure the bowl does not touch the water. Stir gently until melted, then remove from the pan. Scatter the cocoa powder in a flat dish.

4 Using 2 forks, dip the prunes in the melted chocolate, wiping off any excess chocolate on the side of the bowl. Roll them straight in the cocoa powder and place on a clean plate. Allow to set, preferably in a cool place, or otherwise in the fridge. Don't serve straight from the fridge.

More than a snack but less than a proper cake, these bars are nutty and fruity. Wonderful with a strong after dinner coffee.

Raspberry and oat bars

makes 6–8

1 Preheat the oven to 170°C/Gas Mark 3. Lightly grease a 20cm square tin and line it with baking parchment.
2 To make the base, sift together the flour and baking powder. Add the butter, sugar and salt and rub everything together with your fingertips to form crumbs. Stir in the oats. Spread this mixture over the base of the prepared tin; don't press down too much, so the base remains light. Bake for 20 minutes or until light brown. Remove from the oven and allow to cool a little, then spread with the jam.
3 For the topping, place the nuts in a large bowl. In a small saucepan, heat up the butter, sugar, milk and vanilla. Stir until the sugar has dissolved, then pour the mixture over the chopped nuts and stir together. Pack the nut mix evenly over the jam and return to the oven for 30 minutes, until the nuts have turned a nice golden brown.
4 Leave to cool, then remove from the tin and slice into bars or squares.

Base
120g plain flour
⅓ tsp baking powder
100g unsalted butter, diced
60g caster sugar
a pinch of salt
80g whole rolled oats

Filling
220g raspberry jam, bought or homemade ↗ page 276

Topping
70g flaked almonds
70g pecan nuts, roughly chopped
70g hazelnuts, roughly chopped
70g Brazil nuts, roughly chopped
100g unsalted butter
75g caster sugar
40ml milk
1 tsp vanilla essence

Forget their healthy image, our granola bars are as tasty as any rich, sticky snack bar. Children love them and some of our grown-up customers can't go through the whole day without one.

Granola bars

makes 6–8

1 Preheat the oven to 140°C/Gas Mark 1. Lightly grease a 20cm square tin and line it with baking parchment.
2 Scatter the pecans on a baking tray and roast for 8 minutes. Remove from the oven and increase the temperature to 160°C/Gas Mark 3.
3 Half fill a small bowl with hot water and add the apricots and cherries. Leave to soak for about 10 minutes and then drain through a colander.
4 In a large mixing bowl, stir together all the ingredients apart from the butter, honey and sugar. Put these last 3 in a small saucepan and bring to a light simmer. Leave to cook to a light brown colour, watching the whole time so the caramel doesn't spill over or go too dark. Once light brown, pour it over the dry ingredients and stir to mix everything together. Spoon the mixture into the lined tin and pack it down lightly with a palette knife or spoon.
5 Bake for about 22 minutes, until lightly coloured on top. The bar will still be soft when removed from the oven but will firm up as it cools down. Take out of the tin and cut into individual bars. Eat straight away or store in a sealed container.

45g pecan nuts
45g dried apricots,
   very roughly chopped
45g dried sour cherries
45g pumpkin seeds
30g sesame seeds
30g ground almonds
190g whole rolled oats
1¼ tsp ground cinnamon
a pinch of salt
95g unsalted butter
85g honey
95g Demerara sugar

Brownies

The basic principle for a heavenly brownie is getting the baking time right. There is nothing worse than a brownie that turns into a cake. It is worse even than overdone meat. Actually, it is a similar kind of expertise; being able to tell how far to cook a brownie or a sirloin steak is knowledge that comes with time.

When you stick a skewer inside your cooked brownie it must come out covered with lots of gooey crumb, not with dry crumbs, but it mustn't be the type of wet mix you started off with. It should be thicker and sticky to the touch, with a tendency to set once it has cooled down a bit. The brownie should also have risen slightly (10–20 per cent) in the oven and its surface should be totally dry.

The time it takes to reach this stage will vary depending on your oven, where the brownie is placed in it, the size and dimensions of your baking tray and other small variables. So we strongly recommend that you check the brownie well before the indicated baking time has elapsed. If it turns out to be underbaked, chilling it will make it set hard and you will still be able to slice it and enjoy it.

The recipes on page 240 are for a 22cm square tin but you could easily swap that for another tin or dish with a similar surface area or a round cake tin 25cm in diameter.

Macadamia and white chocolate brownies (↗ page 240)

Chapter 3   Baking and patisserie

Khalid's chocolate and chestnut bars (↗ page 241), Toffee brownies (↗ page 240)

Toffee

makes 8–10

1 Start by making the butter toffee. Lightly brush an oven tray (not the one you will use to bake the brownies in) with melted butter. Put the butter and sugar for the toffee in a heavy-based saucepan and place over a medium heat. Stir constantly with a wooden spoon until the mixture turns a dark caramel colour (at one point it might seem the mixture has split; it will come back together when you stir vigorously). Carefully pour the toffee on to the buttered tray and leave aside until it sets.

2 When you are ready to make the brownies, brush a 22cm square baking tin with melted butter and line with baking parchment. Preheat the oven to 170°C/Gas Mark 3. Sift together the flour and salt.

3 Put the butter and chocolate in a heatproof bowl and place over a saucepan of simmering water, making sure the water does not touch the base of the bowl. Leave to melt, stirring from time to time. As soon as the butter and chocolate have melted, remove the bowl from above the water. This is important! You need to avoid getting the mix very hot.

4 In a large bowl, lightly whisk together the eggs, sugar and vanilla. Work them just until combined, a few seconds only, as there is no need to incorporate any air into the eggs. Fold in the melted chocolate mixture and then the sifted flour. Break the toffee into small pieces and fold them in as well.

5 Pour the mix into the lined tin. Drop the jam in spoonfuls into the mixture and swirl it around with a knife.

6 Place on the centre shelf of the oven and bake for roughly 25 minutes. Make sure you check the instructions pn page 236 before deciding to remove the brownie from the oven. Once out, allow it to cool down completely before removing from the tin (you might even need to chill it first). Cut into any shape you like and keep in an airtight container for up to 5 days.

200g unsalted butter, plus melted butter for greasing
280g plain flour
½ tsp salt
300g dark chocolate, broken into pieces
2 free-range eggs
220g caster sugar
1 tsp vanilla essence
140g apricot, banana or raspberry jam ↗ page 276

Butter toffee
25g unsalted butter, plus melted butter for greasing
75g caster sugar

Macadamia and white chocolate

makes 8–10

1 Preheat the oven to 170°C/Gas Mark 3. Spread the nuts out in an ovenproof dish and roast for 5 minutes, then remove from the oven.

2 Follow the brownie instructions in the recipe above up to the stage where you fold in the toffee, adding the instant coffee to the eggs, vanilla and sugar. Instead of the toffee, fold in the white chocolate and half the nuts. Pour the mix into the lined tin and top with the remaining nuts.

3 Continue as in the first brownie recipe.

200g macadamia nuts
200g unsalted butter, plus melted butter for greasing
280g plain flour
½ tsp salt
300g dark chocolate, broken into pieces
2 free-range eggs
230g caster sugar
1 tsp vanilla essence
2 tsp instant coffee
200g white chocolate, broken into pieces (or use chocolate chips)

Decadent is probably the most truthful description of this delicacy. It is both rich and luxurious, with its remarkable mixture of chestnut, fig and chocolate. Soaking the figs in rum or brandy will add an extra dimension. Consider cutting the bars into tiny squares to serve with good coffee at the end of a meal.

You can buy cooked peeled chestnuts, usually tinned or vacuum packed. Avoid the ones cooked in syrup, as they are too sweet for this recipe. If you feel like collecting them, sweet chestnuts fall from the trees in abundance around October (but don't get confused with the horse chestnut, conkers). To prepare them, score each one down one side and place in a saucepan. Cover with boiling water, bring back to the boil and simmer for 15 minutes. Drain and leave until cool enough to handle, then peel away the skins, both outer and inner.

Khalid's chocolate and chestnut bars

makes 8–10

1 Preheat the oven to 150°C/Gas Mark 2. Lightly grease a 20cm square tin and line it with aluminium foil or baking parchment.
2 For the base, place the biscuits in a large bowl and crush with your hands or a rolling pin. Add the melted butter and mix together to make a sandy paste. Scatter this mixture in the tin and press hard on to the base until level. Leave in the fridge to set.
3 Meanwhile, put the dark chocolate and butter in a heatproof bowl set over a saucepan of simmering water and leave to melt. Stir occasionally with a wooden spoon and remove from the pan as soon as they melt so that they don't get too hot.
4 Use an electric mixer to whisk the eggs, yolk and sugar together until thick and pale (if it doesn't scare you, you could also do it with a hand whisk). Gently fold the chocolate mixture into the eggs, followed by the chopped chestnuts, figs and white chocolate. Spread evenly over the biscuit base and bake on the middle shelf of the oven for 15–20 minutes. A skewer inserted in the bar should come out with lots of gooey crumb attached, the same as when you make brownies (see ↗ page 236 for a full description). Make sure you don't go beyond this point. Remove from the oven, leave to cool, then refrigerate for a few hours until set.
5 Take the bar out of the tin and peel off the foil or paper. Cut into bars or squares and dust lightly with cocoa powder. Let them come to room temperature before serving.

225g dark chocolate
150g unsalted butter, diced
2 free-range eggs
1 free-range egg yolk
45g caster sugar
120g cooked peeled chestnuts, roughly chopped
120g dried figs (the soft, ready-to-eat type), stalks removed, roughly chopped
120g white chocolate, roughly chopped
cocoa powder for dusting

Base
190g digestive biscuits
90g unsalted butter, melted

Macaroons

The popularity of these traditional French delicacies has soared over the last few years and they are now seen everywhere. The best ones, admittedly, are made by the Parisian company, Ladurée, which now has a branch at Harrods. We highly recommend going there to sample their classic French patisserie-style macaroons. Our macaroons are more 'homely', as we prefer to keep them as natural as possible. As such, they don't have the same dazzling effect but they are still wonderfully tasty – soft, with a slight crunch, richly flavoured and stunning to look at. Some of the flavour combinations, like Khalid's Lime and basil (↗ page 247), are quirky yet scrumptious.

   Below we give the general method for making macaroons, followed by three variations. Shaping the macaroons does take a bit of skill but even odd-shaped ones will taste great. If you accidentally overbake your macaroons and they go hard, try freezing them, uncovered, for a while before sandwiching them together with the filling. They will absorb moisture and soften a little.

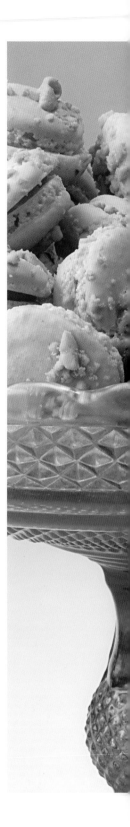

Salty peanut and caramel, Chocolate, and Lime and basil macaroons (↗ page 247)

General method

See the individual macaroon recipes for ingredients.

1 Heat up the oven to 170°C/Gas Mark 3. Using a fine sieve, sift the icing sugar and ground almonds into a clean, dry bowl.

2 Place the egg whites and caster sugar in the bowl of a freestanding electric mixer and start whisking on full speed until the whites have formed a thick, aerated meringue, firm but not too dry. Remove the bowl from the machine, take a third of the meringue and fold it gently into the sifted almond and sugar mix. Once incorporated, add another third of the meringue and continue similarly until all the meringue has been added and the mix appears smooth and glossy.

3 Take a sheet of baking parchment and 'glue' it on to a baking sheet by dotting the tray in a few places with a tiny amount of the macaroon mix. Now you need to use the mix to create uniform shallow discs, about the size of a two-pound coin. In our kitchens we pipe the macaroon mix on to the lined tray using a piping bag fitted with a small nozzle. This requires a bit of experience but you can try it.

4 To assist you, draw little circles on the paper, spaced well apart. This will guide you in achieving consistently sized macaroons. Then either pipe or spoon little blobs of the macaroon mix on to the lined tray. Alternatively, take a bowl of icing sugar, dip your fingers in it and shape the macaroons with your hands.
Now hold the tray firmly and tap its underside vigorously. This should help to spread and smooth out the biscuits. Leave the macaroons out and uncovered for 15 minutes before baking.

5 To bake, place the macaroons in the preheated oven and leave for about 12 minutes. They might take longer, depending on your oven. The macaroons are ready when they come freely off the paper when lifted with a palette knife. Remove from the oven as soon as they reach this stage, so that you don't overbake them, and leave aside to cool down completely.

6 To assemble the macaroons, use a small spoon or a piping bag to deposit a pea-sized amount of the filling on the flat side of half the biscuits. Sandwich them with the other half, squeezing them together gently. Leave at room temperature to set within a couple of hours, or chill them to hasten the process. Just remember not to serve your macaroons cold from the fridge.

This combination was thought up by Carol Brough, whose creativity is imbedded in many of our products. Dulce de leche is available in many supermarkets. Some cooks leave a tin of condensed milk inside a pan of boiling water for many hours to make caramel. Do this at your own peril, though. In theory, the tin could explode.

Salty peanut and caramel

makes about 20

110g icing sugar
60g ground almonds
2 free-range egg whites (60g)
40g caster sugar
20g natural roasted peanuts, roughly chopped

Caramel filling
30g natural roasted peanuts, finely chopped
100g dulce de leche
a pinch of salt

1 To make the macaroons, follow the instructions on page 246, using all the ingredients listed apart from the chopped peanuts. These you add after you have laid out (or piped) the macaroons on the baking tray and before the 15-minute rest. Just dot each biscuit with a few pieces of chopped peanut, leave them to rest, then bake.
2 To make the filling, mix the peanuts with the dulce de leche, stir in a small pinch of salt, then taste. You want to get a sweetness that is balanced by a fair amount of saltiness, a bit like peanut butter.

Lime and basil

makes about 20

110g icing sugar
60g ground almonds
2 free-range egg whites (60g)
40g caster sugar
5 large basil leaves, finely chopped
finely grated zest of 1 lime

Buttercream filling
100g unsalted butter, at room temperature
45g icing sugar
juice and finely grated zest of 1 lime
5 large basil leaves, finely chopped

1 To make the buttercream filling, place the butter and icing sugar in a mixing bowl and beat them together with a rubber spatula until pale in colour and light in texture. Add the lime juice and zest and the basil and beat them in until fully incorporated. Cover the buttercream with cling film and leave in a cool place, but not the fridge.
2 To make the macaroons, follow the instructions on page 246, using all the ingredients listed. Fold the basil and lime zest into the mix at the final stage, after the almonds and icing sugar are fully incorporated into the meringue.

Chocolate

makes about 20

110g icing sugar
50g ground almonds
12g cocoa powder
2 free-range egg whites (60g)
40g caster sugar

Ganache filling
65g dark chocolate
15g unsalted butter
50ml double cream
2 tsp dark rum

1 Start by making the ganache filling. Chop up the chocolate into tiny pieces and the butter into small dice. Place them in a heatproof bowl. Pour the cream into a small saucepan and bring to the boil, watching it carefully. As soon as it boils, pour it over the chocolate and butter. Stir gently with a rubber spatula until you get a smooth mix (if the chocolate doesn't melt easily, help it by placing the bowl over a pot of simmering water and stirring). Stir in the rum until well blended.
2 Place a sheet of cling film over the surface of the ganache and leave to set somewhere cool for a couple of hours. Don't put it in the fridge. It should not get too hard, as you need to spoon it between the macaroons.
3 To make the macaroons, follow the instructions on page 246, using the ingredients listed and adding the cocoa powder to the icing sugar and ground almonds when sifting them.

Meringues

If you ask someone if they've heard of Ottolenghi, the answer is often, 'Yes, I know, it's the place with the meringues'. Though we learned how to make the giant meringues at Baker and Spice, it was our multiflavoured, multicoloured ones (proudly filling our windows) that became synonymous with Ottolenghi and earned us lots of imitators, both good and bad. And now, whether we like it or not, we are identified with those giant balls of sweetness.

To make meringues you need a good freestanding electric mixer. Making them by hand is out of the question and using a handheld electric mixer is also not very practical, as the mixture needs a long whisking time and turns too hard for most weak machines.

Pistachio and rosewater

makes 12 large meringues

600g caster sugar
**300g free-range egg whites
  (about 10)**
2 tsp rosewater ↗ page xii
**60g pistachio nuts,
  finely chopped**

1 Preheat the oven to 200°C/Gas Mark 6. Spread the sugar evenly over a large oven tray lined with baking parchment. Place the tray in the oven for about 8 minutes or until the sugar is hot (over 100°C). You should be able to see it beginning to dissolve at the edges.

2 While the sugar is in the oven, place the egg whites in the bowl of a freestanding electric mixer fitted with the whisk attachment. When the sugar is almost ready, start the machine on high speed and let it work for a minute or so, until the whites just begin to froth up.

3 Carefully pour the sugar slowly on to the whisking whites. Once it has all been added, add the rosewater and continue whisking on high speed for 10 minutes or until the meringue is cold. At this point it should keep its shape when you lift a bit from the bowl and look homogenously silky (you can now taste the mixture and fold in some more rosewater if you want a more distinctive rose flavour).

4 Turn down the oven temperature to 110°C/Gas Mark ¼. To shape the meringues, line a baking tray (or 2, depending on their size) with baking parchment, sticking it firmly to the tray with a bit of meringue. Spread the pistachios over a flat plate.

5 Have ready 2 large kitchen spoons. Use one of them to scoop up a big dollop of meringue, the size of a medium apple, then use the other spoon to scrape it off on to the plate of pistachios. Roll the meringue so it is covered with nuts on one side and then gently place it on the lined baking tray. Repeat to make more meringues, spacing them well apart on the tray. Remember, the meringues will almost double in size in the oven.

6 Place in the preheated oven 110°C and leave there for about 2 hours. Check if they are done by lifting them from the tray and gently prodding to make sure the outside is completely firm, whilst the centre is still a little soft. Remove from the oven and leave to cool. The meringues will keep in a dry place, at room temperature, for quite a few days.

We use the Swiss meringue method here. It involves dissolving the sugars in the egg whites before whipping them up. This enables the brown sugar to mix properly with the whites, creating a uniform mix. Thanks to Carol for making this work, after many trials and tribulations.

Cinnamon and hazelnut

makes 10 large meringues

200g free-range egg whites (about 7)
260g caster sugar
140g dark brown muscovado sugar
½ tsp ground cinnamon
30g unskinned hazelnuts, roughly chopped

1 Preheat the oven to 110°C/Gas Mark ¼.
2 Fill a medium saucepan with water and bring it to a light simmer. Place the egg whites and both sugars in a heatproof bowl large enough to sit on top of the pan. Put it over the simmering water, making sure it doesn't actually touch the water, and leave it there for about 10 minutes, stirring occasionally, until the mixture is quite hot (40°C) and the sugars have dissolved into the whites.
3 Pour into the bowl of a freestanding electric mixer and whip up on high speed, using the whisk attachment. Work the meringue for about 8 minutes or until the mix has cooled down completely. When ready, it should be firm and glossy and keep its shape when you lift a bit with a spoon.
4 Sprinkle the cinnamon over the meringue mix and use a rubber spatula to fold it in gently.
5 Line a flat baking tray (or 2, depending on their size) with baking parchment. You can stick the edges to the tray with a few blobs of the meringue mix. This will hold the paper in place whilst you shape the meringues.
6 Have ready 2 large kitchen spoons. Use one of them to scoop up a generous spoonful of the meringue and the other to scrape this out on to the tray (leave plenty of room between the meringues for them to expand in the oven; they can almost double in size). Using the spoons, shape the meringues into spiky dollops, the size of medium apples, and sprinkle with the chopped hazelnuts. Place in the preheated oven and bake for anything from 1¼–2 hours, depending on the oven and the size of your meringues. To check, poke them gently inside and look underneath. The meringues should be nice and dry underneath and still a little soft in the centre.
7 Remove from the oven and leave to cool. Stored in a dry place, but not the fridge, the meringues will keep for a few days.

Chapter 3 Baking and patisserie

Tartlets

For all the tartlet recipes you will need 6 tartlet tins, 5–7cm in diameter and about 3cm deep. You can use small muffin tins instead or any other tin of similar proportions. Whatever you choose, just make sure you cut out pastry discs that are suitable for the size of your tins. They should be able to cover the bottom and sides of the tin, plus 2–3mm excess to give the tarts extra height.

We recommend making a whole batch of Sweet pastry (↗ page 281) and using as much of it as you need. This will vary according to how large your tins are and how thinly you roll out the pastry. Freeze what is left and keep it for a rainy day.

Pre-baked cases

makes 6

40g melted unsalted butter for brushing
¼–⅓ quantity of Sweet pastry
↗ page 281

plain flour for dusting

1 Start by brushing your tartlet tins with a thin layer of melted butter, then leave to set in the fridge.
2 Meanwhile, prepare a wide, clean working surface and have ready a rolling pin and a small amount of flour. Lightly dust the work surface, place the pastry in the middle and roll out the sweet pastry thinly, turning it around as you go. Work quickly so it doesn't get warm. Once the pastry is no more than 2–3mm thick, cut out 6 circles using a pastry cutter or the rim of a bowl. Line the buttered tins by placing the circles inside and gently pressing them into the corners and sides. Leave to rest in the fridge for at least 30 minutes.
3 Preheat the oven to 150°C/Gas Mark 2. Line each pastry case with a circle of scrunched-up greaseproof paper or a piece of cling film. It should come 1cm above the edge of the pastry (paper muffin cases are another great solution). Fill them up with rice or dry beans, then place in the oven and bake blind for about 25 minutes. By then they should have taken on a golden-brown colour. If they are not quite there yet, remove the beans and lining paper and continue baking for 5–10 minutes. Remove from the oven.
4 Keep the baking beans or rice and the paper holding them for future use. Remove the tart cases from the tins while they are still slightly warm and leave them on the side to cool down completely.

Chapter 3   Baking and patisserie

Fresh berries, Dark chocolate, White chocolate and raspberry tartlets (↗ page 258), Lemon meringue, Banana and hazelnut tartlets (↗ page 259)

Fresh berries

Use a piping bag or a spoon to fill the tart cases three-quarters full with the mascarpone cream. Be creative when topping up generously with the fresh berries. You can throw them on in a beautiful mess or arrange them meticulously – a matter of personality. Dust with icing sugar, if you like, then chill. Serve within 6 hours, but preferably at once.

6 pre-baked tartlet cases
↗ page 255
Mascarpone cream ↗ page 278
50g strawberries, halved or quartered
50g raspberries
50g blueberries
icing sugar for dusting (optional)

Dark chocolate

1 Preheat the oven to 170°C/Gas Mark 3. Put the chocolate and butter in a bowl, set it over a pan of simmering water and leave to melt. Whisk the egg and yolk with the sugar until thick and pale yellow, then fold this into the melted chocolate.
2 If using the jam, put a spoonful in the base of each tartlet case. Fill them up with the chocolate mix; it should reach right up to the rim. Place in the oven and bake for 5 minutes. Cool a little, then remove the tartlets from their tins and allow them to cool down completely.
3 Lightly dust with cocoa powder and serve at room temperature.

150g dark chocolate, broken up
100g unsalted butter, diced
1 free-range egg
1 free-range egg yolk
30g caster sugar
60g raspberry jam (optional) ↗ page 276
6 pre-baked tartlet cases
↗ page 255 **– baked 5 minutes less than suggested and left in their tins**
cocoa powder for dusting

White chocolate and raspberry

1 Crush the fresh raspberries with a fork and then pass them through a fine sieve to remove the pips. Set the smooth coulis aside.
2 Put the white chocolate and the butter in a heatproof bowl. Heat the cream in a small saucepan and bring to the boil, watching it constantly. As soon as it comes to the boil, pour it over the chocolate and butter and stir gently with a rubber spatula. Continue until all the chocolate has melted and you are left with a smooth, shiny ganache.
3 Immediately, before the ganache begins to set, spoon the raspberry jam into the tartlet cases. Carefully pour in the ganache; it should almost reach the rim (if the ganache does begin to set, heat it gently over a pan of hot water before pouring). Be very gentle now and don't shake the cases.
4 Spoon a tiny amount of the raspberry coulis – not more than ½ teaspoon – into the centre of each tart. Use the tip of a knife or a skewer to swirl the coulis around. Carefully transfer the tarts to the fridge and leave them there to set. Remove at least 30 minutes before serving.

40g raspberries
180g white chocolate, chopped into tiny pieces
20g unsalted butter, cut into 5mm dice
90ml double cream
6 tsp raspberry jam, bought or homemade ↗ page 276
6 pre-baked tartlet cases
↗ page 255

Lemon meringue

1   Preheat the oven to 200°C/Gas Mark 6. Spoon the cold lemon curd into the tart cases, filling them three-quarters full. Leave aside, preferably in the fridge.

2   To make the meringue, spread the sugar over an oven tray lined with baking parchment. Place in the hot oven for 5–6 minutes. The sugar should become very hot but mustn't begin to dissolve. Remove from the oven and reduce the temperature to 150°C/Gas Mark 2.

3   At the last minute of heating up the sugar, place the egg whites in the bowl of a freestanding electric mixer. Whisk on high speed for a few seconds, until they begin to froth up. Now carefully pour the hot sugar on to the whisking whites in a slow stream. Once finished, continue whisking for a good 15 minutes, until the meringue is firm, shiny and cold.

4   Use 2 spoons or a piping bag to dispense the meringue on top of the curd and create a pattern. At this point you can either leave the meringue totally white or you can place it in the oven for 1–3 minutes to brown the top very lightly. Serve at once or chill for up to 12 hours.

½ quantity of Lemon curd
↗ page 277 **chilled for at least 6 hours**
6 pre-baked tartlet cases
↗ page 255
120g caster sugar
2 free-range egg whites

Banana and hazelnut

1   Heat the oven to 150°C/Gas Mark 2. Scatter the hazelnuts in an oven tray and roast for 12 minutes. Remove and allow to cool down.

2   While you wait for the nuts, make some burnt butter. Put the butter in a medium pan and cook over a moderate heat. After a few minutes, it should start to darken and smell nutty. Take off the heat and leave to cool slightly.

3   Set aside 10g of the nuts. The rest (plus their skins) put in a food processor, together with 70g of the icing sugar. Work to a fine powder and then add the flour. Pulse together to mix. Add the egg whites and work the machine very briefly, just to mix them in. Repeat with the vanilla and the butter. It is important to stop the machine as soon as the ingredients are incorporated.

4   Mix the mashed banana with the lemon juice and the remaining icing sugar. Spoon about 2 teaspoons of this mixture into each pre-baked tart case (still in its tin). Top with the hazelnut batter. It should come to within 2–3mm of the top. Place in the oven and bake for 20–22 minutes, until the hazelnut filling is completely set. You can check this with a skewer. Remove the tarts from the oven and cool slightly, then carefully remove them from their tins.

5   Put the apricot jam in a small saucepan, stir in a tablespoon of water and bring to the boil. Remove from the heat and brush lightly over the tart tops. Roughly chop the reserved nuts and scatter them on the jam.

6   If using the chocolate, put it in a heatproof bowl and place over a pan of simmering water. Stir gently just until the chocolate melts. Use a spoon to drizzle the tarts gently with the chocolate, trying to create thin, delicate lines. Do not drizzle too much, so the chocolate doesn't take over.

45g unskinned hazelnuts
90g unsalted butter
100g icing sugar
40g plain flour
2 free-range egg whites
½ tsp vanilla essence
50g mashed banana
2 tsp lemon juice
6 pre-baked tartlet cases
↗ page 255 **– baked 5 minutes less than suggested and left in their tins**
50g smooth apricot jam
50g dark chocolate, broken into pieces (optional)

This tart is the pinnacle of comfort. The porridge-like vanilla and semolina filling makes the creamiest, most soothing base, on which the raspberry flavour shines.

Khalid Assyb, who was with us for many years and made a big contribution to our pastry repertoire, came up with the idea. He used to ascribe it, along with many other recipes, to a made-up grandmother. We were all fully aware that this particular grandma had never existed. We loved her anyhow.

Semolina and raspberry tart

serves 4–6

1 Lightly brush an 18cm loose-based cake tin with a tiny amount of oil, then set aside.
2 Make sure you have a clean work surface and a bit of flour to dust it with. Using a rolling pin, roll the pastry out into a rough disc, 2–3mm thick. Work quickly, turning the pastry around as you go. Once you have reached the right thickness, cut the pastry into a circle large enough to cover the tin and most of the sides comfortably. Carefully line the tin, patching up any holes with excess pastry if necessary. When the pastry is in place, use a sharp little knife to trim it so you have a neat edge, roughly 3cm high. Place in the fridge to rest for 30 minutes.
3 Preheat the oven to 170°C/Gas Mark 3. Cut out a circle of baking parchment large enough to cover the base and sides of the cake tin. Place it inside the case and fill up with dry beans or rice so the sides of the pastry are totally supported by the beans and won't collapse during baking. Bake the case blind for 25–35 minutes or until it is very light brown. Remove from the oven and take out the beans or rice (you can keep them for future tarts).
4 To make the filling, put the butter, cream, milk and sugar in a saucepan. Slit the vanilla pod open lengthwise with a sharp knife and scrape out all the flavoursome seeds. Drop the seeds and the scraped pod into the pan. Place the pan on the stove and bring to the boil. Let it simmer while you whisk in the semolina in a slow stream. Continue whisking until the mix comes back to the boil and thickens up like porridge. Remove from the heat and whisk in the egg. Remove the vanilla pod.
5 Pour the semolina mixture into the pastry case and level it with a wet palette knife. Push half the raspberries inside, allowing them to show on the surface. Bake for 20–25 minutes, until the filling is slightly golden. Remove from the oven and cool slightly before removing the tart from the tin.
6 Put the apricot jam in a small pan with a tablespoon of water and bring to the boil. Strain it through a sieve and brush it over the tart. Finish with the remaining raspberries piled over and a dusting of icing sugar.

vegetable oil for brushing the tin
plain flour for dusting
250g Sweet pastry ⌐ page 281
  or use bought pastry
80g unsalted butter
180ml whipping cream
345ml milk
60g caster sugar
½ vanilla pod
60g semolina
1 free-range egg
200g raspberries
50g apricot jam (optional)
icing sugar, to finish

We break away from tradition here. The French clafoutis batter is normally poured over fresh unstoned cherries in a large ovenproof dish, then baked to make a rustic, soufflé-like dessert. Instead, we make stand-alone individual cakes. The reason we include the recipe here rather than in the cake section is that we normally display the clafoutis with similarly shaped tarts to create our vibrant patisserie display.

You can easily revert back to tradition and use a 20cm round or oval baking dish to create a communal plate from which everybody helps themselves to the warm pudding.

Our individual clafoutis can be served warm with ice cream or at room temperature with coffee.

Individual plum clafoutis

makes 6

1 Preheat the oven to 170°C/Gas Mark 3. Take 6 small baking dishes or tins, roughly 10cm in diameter and 2cm deep (ceramic ramekins are a good solution here), and brush them lightly with vegetable oil. Line with baking parchment discs that come 1.5cm above the edge of each dish.
2 Halve the plums, remove the stones and cut each half into 3–4 wedges. Arrange half the fruit over the base of the lined dishes and set the rest aside.
3 To make the batter, whisk the egg yolks with half the sugar until thick and pale. You can do this by hand or with an electric mixer. Use a rubber spatula to fold in first the flour and then the vanilla essence, cream and salt. Slit the vanilla pod open along its length with a sharp knife and scrape out all the seeds, then add them to the batter.
4 Whisk the egg whites with the remaining sugar until they form stiff, but not dry, peaks. Fold them gently into the batter. Pour the batter over the plums to reach about three-quarters of the way up the paper cases. Place in the oven for 15–20 minutes. Take out and quickly arrange the remaining plums on top, slightly overlapping. Continue to bake for about 5 minutes, until a skewer inserted in the centre comes out dry. Allow to cool slightly before removing from the tins. Dust with a little icing sugar, if you like, and serve.

vegetable oil for brushing the tins
4 ripe red plums
3 free-range eggs, separated
70g caster sugar
70g plain flour
1 tsp vanilla essence
150ml double cream
a pinch of salt
½ vanilla pod
icing sugar, to finish (optional)

This makes a substantial treat for an afternoon tea or, served with lightly sweetened crème fraîche, a show-off dessert after a light meal.

You need to make the dough a day in advance (to make your life easier, prepare the mascarpone cream and crumble then, too), then roll it and leave to prove. Assemble and bake close to when you want to serve it. It is best warm.

Brioche galette

serves 4–6

1 After the brioche dough has been in the fridge for 14–24 hours, transfer it to a lightly floured work surface and use a rolling pin to roll it into an oval about 2cm thick (it doesn't need to be perfect). Transfer to a heavy-duty baking tray lightly dusted with flour. Using a pastry brush, lightly brush the rim of the brioche with a small amount of water. Fold in the edge to form a border 1cm thick. Prick all over the centre of the dough with a fork. Cover loosely with cling film and leave somewhere warm until it has risen by about half its volume.

2 Preheat the oven to 170°C/Gas Mark 3. When the brioche has risen sufficiently, brush the edges with a little milk. Spread the centre with the mascarpone cream, being careful not to press down too hard. Scatter the plum slices over the cream and then arrange the berries on top. Brush the berries with the melted butter. Mix the crumble with the almonds and cinnamon and sprinkle on top.

3 Bake in the preheated oven for 25–30 minutes. Check the base by lifting with a palette knife to make sure it is evenly coloured. Transfer to a wire rack and leave to cool slightly.

4 Just before serving, scoop out the inside of the passion fruit and drizzle it over the fruits.

1 quantity of Brioche dough
↗ page 177
plain flour for dusting
milk for brushing
⅓ quantity of Mascarpone cream
↗ page 278
1 red plum, halved, stoned and cut into slices about 2mm thick
150g mixed berries (e.g. raspberries, blackcurrants, blueberries)
30g slightly salted butter, melted
¼ quantity of Crumble ↗ page 279
15g flaked almonds
1 tsp ground cinnamon
1 ripe passion fruit

Larder

The sky's the limit when it comes to tahini. It works in total harmony with roasted or fresh vegetables, with grilled fish or with barbecued meat. When making it into a sauce, make sure to adjust the amount of liquid according to the brand you use. The sauce should be thick but runny, almost like honey. Once chilled it will thicken, so you will need to whisk it again and possibly add more water.

Green tahini sauce

1 In a bowl, thoroughly whisk the tahini, water, lemon juice, garlic and salt together. The mixture should be creamy and smooth. If it is too thick, add more water. Stir in the chopped parsley, then taste and add more salt if needed.

2 If using a food processor or a blender, process together all the ingredients except the parsley until smooth. Add more water if needed. Add the parsley and turn the machine on again for a second or two. Taste for seasoning.

150ml tahini paste ↗ page xii
150ml water
80ml lemon juice
2 garlic cloves, crushed
½ tsp salt
30g flat-leaf parsley, finely chopped if making by hand

Labneh is an Arab cheese made by straining yoghurt so it loses most of its liquid. Use natural goat's milk yoghurt or, if unavailable, natural full-fat cow's milk yoghurt, but not the set or Greek varieties.

This recipe takes at least 48 hours to make. If this is all too much, you can buy labneh from Middle Eastern grocer's shops. If you do want to venture into this cheesy territory, you can store the labneh in the fridge to use as a spread, like any cream cheese. A more labour-intensive option is to roll it into balls and then preserve them in a jar of oil. The jar will look beautiful, the cheese keeps for weeks at room temperature and the balls will create a special visual effect when used, as they are, in salads and pulse dishes (↗ Couscous and mograbiah with oven-dried tomatoes on page 77).

Labneh

1 Line a large bowl with a piece of muslin or other fine cloth. In another bowl, mix the yoghurt and salt well. Transfer the yoghurt to the muslin, pick up the edges of the cloth and tie them together well to form a bundle. Hang this over your sink or over a large bowl and leave for 48 hours. By this time the yoghurt will have lost most of its liquid and be ready to use as a spread.

2 To go the whole hog, leave it hanging for a day longer. Remove the labneh from the cloth and place in a sealed container in the fridge. Once it is thoroughly chilled, preferably after 24 hours, roll the cheese into balls, somewhere between the size of an olive and a walnut.

3 Take a sterilised jar about 600ml in capacity (see Preserved lemons, opposite, for how to sterilise jars). Pour some of the oil inside and gently lay the balls in the oil. Add some more oil and continue with the balls until all the cheese is inside and immersed in the oil. Seal the jar and keep until needed.

4 Before serving, scatter the mint and pepper on a flat plate and roll the labneh balls in it.

1 litre natural goat's milk yoghurt (or full-fat cow's milk yoghurt)
¾ tsp salt
200–300ml olive oil
10–15g dried mint
a good grind of black pepper

The preserving process will take a few weeks, starting with just the lemon and salt and later adding the rest. The same method can be used with limes.

Preserved lemons

1. Before starting, get a jar just large enough to accommodate all the lemons tightly. To sterilise it, fill it up with boiling water, leave for a minute and then empty it. Allow it to dry out naturally without wiping it so it remains sterilised.
2. Wash the lemons and cut a deep cross all the way from the top to 2cm from the base, so you are left with 4 quarters attached. Stuff each lemon with a spoonful of salt and place in the jar. Push the lemons in tightly so they are all squeezed together well. Seal the jar and leave for at least a week.
3. After this initial period, remove the lid and press the lemons as hard as you can to squeeze as much of the juice out of them as possible. Add the rosemary, chilli and lemon juice and cover with a thin layer of olive oil. Seal the jar and leave in a cool place for at least 4 weeks. The longer you leave them, the better the flavour.

6 unwaxed lemons
6 tbsp coarse sea salt
2 sprigs of rosemary
1 large red chilli
juice of 6 lemons
olive oil

This recipe has almost reached the sphere of mythology, due to the anticipation involved every time Yotam goes to Israel, before he comes back with a bag full of jars containing his mother's famous mayonnaise. Well here it is, the legendary recipe, and it makes the best addition to a grilled chicken and tomato sandwich.

Ruth's mayonnaise

1. The best way to make this mayonnaise is by using a stick blender. You could also use a food processor or liquidiser, or make it by hand, using a whisk. If doing it by hand, you need to crush the garlic and chop the coriander finely before you start.
2. If using a stick blender, put the egg, mustard, sugar, salt, garlic and vinegar in a large mixing bowl. Process a little and then start adding the oil in a slow trickle. Keep the machine working as you pour in a very light stream of oil. Once the mayonnaise starts to thicken, you can increase the stream until all the oil is fully incorporated. Now add the coriander and continue processing until it is all chopped and properly mixed in. Transfer to a clean jar and chill. The mayonnaise will keep in the fridge for up to 2 weeks.

1 free-range egg
¾ tbsp Dijon mustard
2 tsp caster sugar
½ tsp salt
3 garlic cloves, peeled
2 tbsp cider vinegar
500ml sunflower oil
15g fresh coriander,
  leaves and stalks

This is extremely useful for pouring over cakes, fruit salads, pavlovas
– anything sweet, really. Only use passion fruit that are nice and ripe; that
is when their skin turns dark brown and starts to shrivel.

Passion fruit jam

1 Halve the passion fruit and use a spoon to scoop out the pulp straight
   into a small saucepan. Add the sugar, stir well with a wooden spoon
   and put over a low heat. Bring to a slow simmer and cook for about
   5 minutes, stirring frequently and taking great care that it doesn't stick
   to the bottom of the pan. When ready, it should be as thick as honey.
   To make sure, chill a little bit of the jam in a bowl in the fridge and
   check its consistency.
2 Once ready, pour into a clean jar, leave to cool completely, then seal
   and store in the fridge. The jam will keep for at least 2 weeks.

**300g passion fruit pulp
(roughly 10 passion fruit)
150g caster sugar**

Not quite a jam but somewhere in between a jam and a coulis, this
is extremely handy in many cakes and sweets. The tartness of the
raspberry cuts the sweetness and balances it. The raspberry seeds
add fruitiness and freshness.

You can flavour the jam with vanilla or star anise. Just add ½ vanilla
pod or 2 star anise while cooking.

Raspberry jam

Put the raspberries and sugar in a small, heavy-bottomed saucepan
and stir them together. Put over a low heat, bring to a light simmer and
cook for 7–8 minutes. Remove from the heat, transfer to a bowl, cover
the surface with cling film, leave to cool and then refrigerate.

**300g raspberries
100g caster sugar**

Lemon curd

1 Put all the ingredients in a large, heavy-based saucepan, leaving out roughly half the butter. Place over a medium heat and, using a hand whisk, whisk constantly while you cook the curd. Reduce the heat if it starts sticking to the bottom of the pan. Once the curd reaches boiling point, you will notice large bubbles coming to the surface. Continue whisking vigorously for another minute and then remove from the heat.

2 Off the heat, add the remaining butter and whisk until it has melted. Pass the curd through a sieve and into a plastic container. Cover the surface with cling film, allow it to come to room temperature and then chill for at least 6 hours, preferably overnight, for it to firm up well. It will keep in the frige for up to 4 days.

200ml lemon juice (4–6 lemons)
grated zest of 4 lemons
200g caster sugar
4 free-range eggs
4 free-range egg yolks
180g unsalted butter,
  cut into cubes

Vanilla essence

Use a small, sharp knife to slit the vanilla pods open along their length, then scrape the seeds out with the tip of the knife. Place the seeds and pods in a medium saucepan, cover with the water and sugar and bring to the boil. Boil rapidly for about 15 minutes, until the essence has reduced to a third of its original volume. Pour into a jar and leave to cool, then seal with a tight-fitting lid. Keep refrigerated for up to a month.

4 vanilla pods
500ml water
120g caster sugar

This cream makes a very versatile condiment. It is heavenly with fresh berries or roasted fruit and goes incredibly well with a cake just out of the oven (try with Peach and raspberry teacakes, page 206). If you have a spice grinder, consider substituting ¼ teaspoon of ground star anise for the vanilla.

Mascarpone cream

1 Put the mascarpone in a mixing bowl and loosen it up with a whisk. Add the rest of the ingredients and continue whisking until the cream thickens up again. It should be able to hold its shape when lifted with a spoon. Chill until ready to use.

110g mascarpone cheese
110ml crème fraîche
¼ tsp vanilla essence ↗ page 277
25g icing sugar

Crumble

1 Put the flour, sugar and butter in a bowl and mix with your hands or an electric mixer fitted with the beater attachment to work it to a uniform breadcrumb consistency. Make sure there are no lumps of butter left. If using a mixer, watch it carefully. Within a few seconds, a crumble can turn into a cookie dough. (If this unpleasant scenario happens, roll it out thinly, cut out cookies, bake them and half dip in melted chocolate.)
2 Transfer the crumble to a plastic container. It will keep in the fridge for up to 5 days, or for ages in the freezer.

300g plain flour
100g caster sugar
200g cold unsalted butter,
   cut into small cubes

There is nothing more satisfying than making your own granola. We give you poetic licence to add any of your favourite nuts, fruit or seeds.

Granola

1 Preheat the oven to 140°C/Gas Mark 1. Roughly chop all the nuts and put them in a large mixing bowl. Add the oats and seeds and set aside.
2 Mix together all the syrup ingredients in a small saucepan. Place over a low heat and stir while you warm the syrup gently. Once it is warm, pour it over the seeds, nuts and oats and stir well with a wooden spoon.
3 Line a large baking tray with baking parchment and spread the granola over it evenly. It should form a layer no more than 1cm thick. If it is too thick, consider using 2 trays. Bake for 40 minutes, turning and mixing the granola 2 or 3 times. When ready, it will have taken on a dark, honey-like colour. Don't worry if it is soft; once it is cool it will turn crunchy. Remove from the oven. While the granola is still warm, but not hot, stir in the fruit. Leave to cool on the tray and then transfer to a sealed container. It will keep for up to 2 weeks.

60g whole unskinned almonds
40g Brazil nuts
40g cashew nuts
300g whole rolled oats
60g pumpkin seeds
60g sunflower seeds
100g dried apricots, roughly
   chopped
60g dried cranberries
60g dried blueberries

Syrup
¼ tsp salt
3 tbsp water
2 tbsp rapeseed oil
2 tbsp sunflower oil
120ml maple syrup
120ml honey

Making your own puff pastry is definitely a challenge. This recipe isn't so difficult but we won't hold it against you if you choose to buy your puff. To upgrade a commercial variety, brush it with plenty of melted butter before baking.

Rough puff pastry

1 Sift the flour and salt into a large mixing bowl. Use a coarse cheese grater to grate 80g of the frozen butter into the flour. Lightly mix together. Add the cold water and, using a knife, stir the flour and water together until a dough starts to form. Now use your hands to bring it together into a ball. You may need to add a little more water if some dry bits remain in the bowl. Press the dough into a neat square, wrap it in cling film and chill for 30 minutes.

2 Using a rolling pin, roll out the pastry on a lightly floured work surface into a rectangle with a long edge that is 3 times its width. Grate the remaining butter and spread it evenly over two-thirds of rectangle. Take the third that is not scattered with butter and fold it over on to the middle of the buttered part. Then fold the 2 layers over the remaining single layer. You will be left with 3 layers of pastry and 2 layers of butter separating them.

3 Turn the pastry by 90 degrees. Dust your work surface lightly with flour and roll out the pastry again into a long rectangle with the same proportions as before. The 2 short edges will reveal the 3 layers of pastry and 2 layers of butter.

4 Take one of the short sides and fold it over to reach the middle of the remaining part of the pastry. Fold the remaining third on top of the first one to get 3 layers on top of each other. Wrap the pastry in cling film and rest in the fridge for 30 minutes.

5 Roll the pastry again into a rectangle with the short edges displaying the seams. Fold into 3 as before. Rest in the fridge again for 30 minutes.

6 Repeat the process one last time and then wrap and chill for at least an hour.

7 The pastry will keep in the fridge for up to 4 days and in the freezer for a month.

300g plain flour
1 tsp salt
180g unsalted butter, frozen
140ml ice-cold water

Shortcrust pastry

1 Put the flour and salt into a bowl and add the butter. Rub it in by hand, or using a mixer fitted with the beater attachment, until you reach a fine breadcrumb texture. A third easy option is to use a food processor.
2 Add the water and continue working just until the dough comes together. Stop at once. Shape the pastry into a disc roughly 4cm thick, wrap it in cling film and chill for at least 2 hours.
3 The pastry will keep in the fridge for 5 days and for at least a month in the freezer. Defrost in the fridge overnight.

300g plain flour
½ tsp salt
160g cold unsalted butter, cut into 1cm dice
70ml ice-cold water

Sweet pastry

1 Put the flour, icing sugar, lemon zest and salt in a bowl and add the butter. Rub it in with your hands or, more easily, using a mixer fitted with the beater attachment. Or you can do the job in a food processor. In all cases, you need to mix the ingredients until you get a coarse breadcrumb consistency, making sure there aren't any large lumps of butter left.
2 Add the egg yolk and water and mix just until the dough comes together, being careful not to mix any longer than necessary. You might need to add a tiny amount of extra water.
3 Remove the dough from the mixing bowl and knead very lightly for a few seconds only, just to shape it into a smooth disc, 5–6cm thick. Wrap in cling film and chill until ready to use. The pastry will keep in the fridge for a week and at least a month in the freezer.

330g plain flour
100g icing sugar
grated zest of ½ lemon
¼ teaspoon salt
180g cold unsalted butter, cut into small cubes
1 free-range egg yolk
2 tbsp cold water

Index

The Ottolenghi people

Trying to tell the Ottolenghi story always ends up being the story of the individuals who have participated in forming it. We can only mention here a few of the many who contributed over the years. We are deeply thankful to all the others.

First, Noam Bar, who is a senior partner in the company and has the exceptional combination of an acute business understanding and the ability to grasp the vision and drive us all forward with it.

Second, Cornelia Staeubli, a partner and general manager, the people's person and the one who, incredibly, holds it all together, physically and spiritually.

Then (in rough order of appearance at Ottolenghi): Jim Webb – creative force, manager of all projects, a man of infinite talents; Khalid Assyb – grand chef de pâtisserie; Lingchee Ang – master of the pastries and the pastry counter; Mariusz Uszakiewicz – head baker, ex-footballer and original thinker; Tamar Shany – gifted chef and star of all musicals; Nicole Steel – service provider of the year and the one with the most leaving dos; Francis Pereira – the real manager of Notting Hill; Daniela Geatti – manager, and mother of the first Ottolenghi baby; Alejandra Chavero – the one who brought Ottolenghi standards to Mexico with a big smile; Diana Daniel-Thomas – miraculously manages to put our accounts in order; Reka Fabian – person of details and great devotion; Dan Lepard – the magician who always sorts out our bread; Etti Mordo – passionately original chef with rare execution; Colleen Murphy – head pastry chef, head chef and our token East Ender; Tricia Jadoonanan – gifted, good humoured and a commander of many manly chefs; Marketa Kratochvilova – the brilliantly artistic arranger of the display; Emma Christian – efficient catering princess; Danielle Postma – creative culinary star with many admirers; Ramael Scully – the calmest and one of the most consistently inspired chefs; Jason Chuck – a sportsman and a chef who never gets dirty; Erica Rossi – Italian energy bomb and Camden town beloved; Maria Oskarsson – the only person in the world who managed to get into Cornelia's shoes; Helene Sauvage – assistant manager and a Notting Hill star with French elegance; Nguyo Milcinovic – our evening star and Scully's right hand man; Tal Kimchi – great kitchen organiser and a multi-talent; Karl Allen – the customers' favourite manager; Carol Brough – patient cake maker and inventor; Helen Goh – creator, perfectionist and analyst of a rare kind; Nir Feller – fiery foodie and bohemian; Marina Dos Santos – the one who brought us Continental chic and restaurant zeal; Gerard Viccars – meticulous and conscientious chef, plus a few tattoos; Sara Lee – the quality guard and promoter of wonderful packed products; Arek Karas – ultimate problem solver and computer wiz; Sara Fereidooni – a serious manager with an infectious charm; Basia Murphy – living proof that you can be an effective manager and smile; Itamar Strulovich – a rising talent of food and wit; Sarit Packer – merry mistress of the pastry department.

Thank yous

Big thanks to Alex Meitlis and Tirza Florentin, not so silent partners, whom, in two opposite departments, had a huge part in moulding Ottolenghi.

We would like to thank Amos Oppenheim for his limitless trust and generosity. His constant smile is deeply missed. And thank you to the others who had early faith: Tamara Meitlis, Ariela Oppenheim, David Oppenheim, Itzik and Ilana Lederfeind, Danny Florentin, Keren Margalit and Yoram Ever-Hadani.

For making this book happen, infinite thanks to Felicity Rubinstein and Sarah Lavelle; for making it so breathtakingly beautiful, thanks to Axel Feldmann, Sam Wolfson, Richard Learoyd and Adam Laycock; and for taking care of the details, thanks to Jane Middleton.

For the spectacular dishes and plates used in the photography, we are indebted to Lindy Wiffen from Ceramica Blue. And thanks to Gerry Ure for smiling through the hassle.

For precious assistance in making the recipes work: Jim Webb, Alison Quinn, Claudine Boulstridge, Marianne Lumb and Philippa Shepherd.

And more warm thanks, for many different reasons, to: Charley Bradley, Leigh Genis, Dino Cura, Paul and Ossi Burger, Adrien von Ferscht, Tamasin Day-Lewis, Patricia Michelson, Sarah Bilney, Binnie Dansby, Patrick Houser, Caroline Waldegrave, Jenny Stringer, Viv Pidgeon, Max Clark, Sue Spaull, Gail Mejia, Dariusz Przystasz, Przemek Suszek, Karen Handler-Kremmerman, Dorit Mintzer, Sigal Baranowitz, Pete and Greta Allen, and Jenny and Tony Taylor.

Thank you to all our devoted suppliers, without whom the wheels of the machine would not be turning.

And most humble thanks to all the Ottolenghi customers, the ultimate source of our pleasure and livelihood.